WOMEN
OF
OPUS DEI

IN THEIR OWN WORDS

WOMEN
OF
OPUS DEI

IN THEIR OWN WORDS

**M. T. Oates, Linda Ruf,
and Jenny Driver, MD**

A Crossroad Book
The Crossroad Publishing Company
New York

In continuation of our two-hundred-year tradition of independent publishing, Crossroad proudly offers a variety of books with strong, original
voices and perspectives on topics from spirituality and counseling to public theology and human sexuality. The viewpoints expressed in our books
are not necessarily those of Crossroad or its employees.

The Crossroad Publishing Company
16 Penn Plaza – 481 Eighth Avenue, Suite 1550
New York, NY 10001

Printed in the United States of America.

The text of this book is set in 11/14.5 Activa.
The display face is Benguiat Gothic.

Library of Congress Cataloging-in-Publication Data
Women of Opus Dei : in their own words / edited by M.T. Oates,
Linda Ruf, and Jenny Driver.
    p. cm.
  ISBN-13: 978-0-8245-2425-8 (alk. paper)
  ISBN-10: 0-8245-2425-X (alk. paper)
  1. Opus Dei (Society) 2. Opus Dei (Society) – Biography. 3. Women
in the Catholic Church – Biography. I. Oates, M. T. (Marie T.), 1962-
II. Ruf, Linda. III. Driver, Jenny, M.D. IV. Title.
BX819.3.O68W66 2008
267′.182082 – dc22

                        2008045317

1 2 3 4 5 6 7 8 9 10   14 13 12 11 10 09

Contents

Foreword

by Susan Mangels,
President of Lexington College, Chicago

Although the title of this book mentions Opus Dei, the personal stories contained in this book are, more than anything else, stories of personal conversion to Jesus Christ. These are not stories of perfect women without their daily struggles and their personal defects. The women in this book are just like all women. These are true stories about a variety of women who have found and committed themselves to a personal relationship with Jesus Christ — all through traditional Catholic prayer, practices, and beliefs. The women in this book appear content with and well-versed in their faith. I would even say they come across as in love and passionate about it. Given some of the difficulties the Catholic Church has faced in recent years, some may find this fidelity and excitement about one's faith striking, perhaps even oxymoronic. Reading these stories reminded me of my own story and how a few women in love with their faith led me closer to Christ.

Over twenty years ago, when I was still a practicing Lutheran, I was interested in the Catholic Church, but as a historical and cultural phenomenon. I had never heard of the personal prelature called Opus Dei. As a young child I was raised to be an involved and practicing Lutheran. Faith was good. The key points of our family belief focused on honoring and loving God, and church was one more activity in my life. Like so many young people then and today, as I became a teenager I pulled away from good Christian virtue in some areas of my life. I became pro-choice, though certainly not all Lutherans are pro-choice. I ended up going to a Baptist college and, as fate would have it, I was given one of the few Catholics on campus as one of my roommates, along with a Baptist roommate. Both were strong in their faith and love of God and were good role models for me. They both helped me to continue practicing as a Protestant.

Once exposed to it, though, I admit that I was immediately attracted to the elegance and liturgy of the Catholic Church; it reminded me of my childhood Lutheran Church.

Moreover, my Catholic roommate impressed me with her commitment to get to Mass every Sunday even if she had been at a party late the night before, and her pro-life rationale slowly won me over. Through friendship, she and her mother — a supernumerary member of Opus Dei — basically challenged my intellect and will with their fervent Catholicism. Our conversations formed a big part of my intellectual growth during our four years together at college. I loved it!

Our deep conversations occurred as I took courses in my undergraduate major of art history and looked more closely at Martin Luther's legacy and teachings. The former led me to believe the Protestant split was more than anything else unfortunate, and the latter helped me realize Luther's body of work did not add up when contrasted with the Catholic Church's teachings and history right at the time of Christ.

Centuries of art and architecture inspired largely by Catholic faith brought me to appreciate the beauty of faith and Church history. While some critics prefer to focus on particular questionable events in Catholic Church history, I was impressed when I really looked more thoroughly at the role of the Church, taken as a whole, throughout history. I found that integrity, faith, and reason hung together.

I was also struck when I considered that there are many "fallen-away" Catholics, but I had never met anyone who claimed to be a fallen-away Lutheran. Why did the Catholic Church seem to "stick" with people? This helped lead me to the truth/reality that the Catholic Church was the one true Church.

I read much about what the Church taught and its core doctrinal points before I received the gift of faith to convert. So when the faith came (quietly), it was clear I had a choice to say yes or no. I came to realize that I should either enter the Catholic Church or I would probably live the rest of my life as a cultural Christian. The Catholic Church would be challenging for me to live in, but it was all of a piece. Its teachings had integrity, even if — like all churches — it was made up of sinners.

But if I wanted to go ahead with the beauty I had seen that was now obvious for me intellectually and aesthetically, I had to become a Catholic. The next part of my story, however, took a trajectory I never could have imagined for myself.

Since I found my Catholic faith through persons close to or in Opus Dei, I was familiar with Opus Dei. I even thought I might have a vocation to Opus Dei, because I liked that it could provide me with a framework of traditional Catholic practices and spiritual support from the committed faithful of Opus Dei. Sometime after I converted, I became engaged to be married. All the while, I grew in my new faith and received ongoing Christian formation with Opus Dei.

Several of my friends in Opus Dei at the time were numerary members, that is, celibate women. I had never conceived that I could ever have a celibate vocation. In fact, I'd never had any interest in the idea. Now I was engaged to be married and was preparing for my wedding. I was thinking that I might have a vocation to be a member who could eventually get married, commonly referred to as a supernumerary. When someone mentioned that perhaps I should think about the possibility of having a celibate calling, I was aghast. I had other plans. I asked God, if this was what he wanted of me (and I was sure he *didn't*), that he make it really obvious.

The more I prayed, the more God let me see that against all that made sense in my life, or so I thought at the time, he was asking me to say yes to trying to be numerary. I broke off my engagement (and upset my family) to take the plunge. But I knew that it was God's idea to try it and that if I didn't make the right choice, I wouldn't have peace.

It must have been what God had planned, though, because I have had peace since the day I said yes in 1988.

Reading the stories in this book reminded me of my own unlikely and yet fulfilling path in the Catholic Church. One of the things I love about the Catholic Church teachings, and which I do not think is well enough understood in our society today, is that women are equal to men, but they are not the same. As St. Josemaría noted, women have special insights that are valuable and needed in all sectors of professional work. I find Opus Dei's emphasis on this Catholic teaching extends radical equality to people in whatever work they do daily. All work has value and is important in God's eyes, especially work that has people caring for each other's well-being.

As president of Lexington College in Chicago, I work hard with my team to communicate that message of both equality and difference to the women who attend our college, which happens to be the only all-women hospitality management college in the United States. It is the only accredited college linked to Opus Dei in the United States at this time. The Prelature of Opus Dei provides the spiritual and pastoral assistance to maintain and develop Lexington's Christian identity. It's truly rewarding to be able to open horizons for young women with regard to how they can make a difference in people's lives through service to others and by truly celebrating their own dignity as professionals in the process.

I was pleased to see included in this book stories of some Lexington College graduates who now work as professionals in the hospitality industry. It makes sense — given Opus Dei's take on the dignity of all work and the radical equality of all workers — that their stories appear alongside those of a tenured university professor, stay-at-home moms, doctors, teachers, a high-level corporate executive, a childcare provider, and others. Taken as a whole, all the narratives in their variety will give readers a good insight into what it means to be a woman in Opus Dei.

Acknowledgments

We would like to thank all the people who participated in this project and helped make this book possible. We are grateful for the support and encouragement we received from the leadership team that oversees the women's programs of Opus Dei in the United States, in particular Mary Elise Eckman and Tona Varela, who assisted us in gaining access to the different women featured in this book and provided us with helpful feedback as we developed the manuscript. We are also grateful to Natalie Barton, who helped us with editing and transcription support. We want to thank Audio File Solutions in Colorado (*www.audiofilesolutions.com*), which provided most of our transcription services for the interviews in the book. We are also very grateful to Theodora Simons and Mary Alice Teti, who served as critical readers of the manuscript. We want to thank Julia Boles and Patricia Keefe, who were also interviewed for this book. We are thankful to Nancy Neal and John Eagleson at Crossroad for their work in preparing the manuscript. Of course, we also want to thank our families, whose ongoing support and affection help make all of our efforts more possible, lovable, and fruitful.

Preface

by Barbara Kay, Columnist
for the *National Post* of Canada

My job as a weekly opinion columnist brings me into contact, usually only electronically, with some truly fascinating people. Occasionally this leads to an actual meeting for an interview or collaboration around a subject of mutual interest. On rare occasions a meeting blossoms into a friendship. And once I fell into a friendship with a reader that so enriched my life that it led to the honor of being asked to write the preface to this book.

In the fall of 2005, I received an e-mail from Monique David, a first-time correspondent, inviting me to speak the following February to a group of high school girls taking part at a conference near Montreal. The students, this e-mail explained, would be participating in an intensive program aimed at developing leadership skills. As a "role model," I was to speak to them on a personal level, that is, reflect on the values and choices that had influenced my life's trajectory. I was also to talk about the profession of journalism, and in particular my domain of critical commentary.

The invitation both flattered and intrigued me. This Monique David had no way of knowing that I was, at the age of sixty-two, a newcomer to the profession, having taken up my job at Canada's *National Post* newspaper a mere two years earlier. Hers was the first such invitation I had been offered, and the implied compliment — that the ideas and points of view expressed in my columns were worthy of emulation by a group of ambitious girls on the threshold of adult life — came as an extremely validating early response to the niche I was still in the process of carving out.

I accepted the invitation with alacrity, but with only a vague understanding of what exactly the Foundation for Culture and Education, which administered the conference center Monique represented, was all about. In fact, as our first meeting approached, I began to worry a bit: the name of the foundation gave no hint of its sponsorship. Was I being co-opted by a political organization with dubious goals? I hoped that my vanity had not led me into a potentially embarrassing situation.

Any anxiety, however, was quickly laid to rest the moment I met Monique. A woman of particular charm and poise — and some other hard-to-define but assuring quality — told me I was dealing with a transparent individual of absolute integrity. The foundation she worked for clearly stood for something good and honorable. Our earliest discussions reassured me that we were, in terms of our social and cultural values, on the same page.

Still, my inability to "place" Monique continued to pique my curiosity. I admit to a certain vanity regarding my competence at what I call social ratiocination, but here was a woman who eluded common female stereotypes.

It wasn't long before I had my answer, when Monique finally told me she was an Opus Dei numerary and director of the women's programs of Opus Dei in Canada. She explained all this with a certain delicate alertness, as though she might find herself dealing with a moment of negative tension and even a halt to further intimacy.

Monique's hesitancy in sharing this crucial part of her identity resonated with me. As a Jew, I have played out this same ever-so-slightly watchful scenario on innumerable occasions. Even among the most educated and modern of people, reflexive prejudices linger, and one can't assume that one will be automatically accepted as a social peer.

I never thought that I would share this instinctive diffidence with a Catholic woman, or any Christian, really. I take for granted that, Christianity being the default religion of Western civilization, nobody sheltered under that wide umbrella could ever regard his or her religious identity as an impediment to social rapport.

At the same time, although I knew very little about Opus Dei and had not formed any particular point of view, I was aware that this Catholic — society? organization? (I wasn't really sure at the time), burdened by the mass obsession around the odiously defamatory novel *The Da Vinci Code*, had been caught up in a most distressing public swirl of controversy. Negative stereotypes of secrecy, elitism, and sinister-sounding rituals hovered around the name.

Many of the rumors, however, seemed to me to carry the same whiff of instinctive baseless malice I associate with anti-Semitism, which naturally inclined me more to skepticism toward Opus Dei's critics than toward Opus Dei itself. And so I look back at that slight hesitancy on Monique's part in revealing her association with Opus Dei as the moment of mutual recognition that cemented our initial bond of friendship.

Since that time our personal camaraderie has flourished. Monique and I have enjoyed many animated conversations about Christianity and Judaism — her faith and my culture. On the surface, our perspectives could not be more polarized: Monique has embraced a vocation in the Work, a faith-based calling predicated on a deep personal relationship with God. I am what any theologian would call an intellectual agnostic. (I often describe my position — only partly tongue in cheek — as that of a believer, but with God's understanding that we will respect each other's privacy.) At the same time I am existentially rooted in a deep emotional and cultural engagement with Jewish peoplehood, the synagogue's traditional liturgy, and Israel's unique destiny.

And yet, oddly enough, we found we agreed on the one critical factor that we believe is fundamental to the very meaning of religion, whether it is theologically or sociologically embraced: we both believe that the natural yearning to transcend the human estate cannot be realized if it is arbitrarily compartmentalized into mere daily or weekly blocks of scheduled prayer and reflection. If the moral demands of a religion are to be fully met, and holiness sought, then one must strive for a state of constant spiritual intention: one's faith must be organically integrated into every minute of the day, every deed one performs, every decision one makes, and every standard one sets for behavior and achievement. This understanding of religion, which hinges on the word "organic," is, as I understand it, the formative principle of Opus Dei.

I don't think it is a coincidence that, as Monique told me, her Jewish friends have grasped the Opus Dei difference quite readily. For Judaism is as well a holistic moral system: there may be a wide intellectual divergence between the observant and the nonobservant, the believing and the still-seeking, but the divine imperative to pursue holiness through righteous aspiration and behavior — Opus Dei's purpose in microcosm — is the bedrock of an authentic Jewish life as well. In neither perspective can this imperative be temporally or conditionally segregated into disparate "religious" and "secular" categories.

In the past two years, thanks to the "networking" effect in meeting some of Monique's fellow members, I have had many opportunities to see the Opus Dei philosophy in action. I have visited four Opus Dei centers in Montreal alone, as well as centers in Ottawa, Quebec City, Jerusalem, and of course Opus Dei's magnificent United States headquarters, in Murray Hill, New York City.

Whether the presenting edifice is that of a simple middle-class home, a stately converted mansion, or a gleaming multi-storied tower; whether its windows look out onto a bourgeois suburban neighborhood, a leafy mountain park, minarets, ancient stone walls and golden cupolas, or soaring skyscrapers, the *habitus,* as philosopher Pierre Bourdieu would call it, of the women within is remarkably uniform.

What you first notice, and what pervades the atmosphere in any Opus Dei center, is a sense of order. Opus Dei's success with young people springs from the knowledge that youth craves freedom but is easily confused and defeated by freedom without boundaries. Our society's worst social ills are the result of the insistence on young people's "rights" to freedom without constraint. What Opus Dei knows is that internal liberty and external structure within whose boundaries free will can be most effectively galvanized, work together to promote the optimal environment for healthy self-realization. Order in matters both spiritual and temporal provides that structure, which in turn produces the atmosphere of calm and reassurance that young people need, but today so rarely find.

Everything in an Opus Dei center is adequate to its purpose, yet does not exceed its purpose. Furnishings are comfortable and harmonious, but not luxurious. Respect for occasion and the aesthetic sensibility of others is evident in their outward personal appearance, which is both modest and modish. For these women embrace their femininity rather than suppress it. They delight in nature's gifts of beauty and grace. And they love to laugh (which suits me, since I love to make people laugh). Their ready humor expresses their friendliness to the world. And yet the observant witness is equally struck by an air of dignified reserve that speaks to a defining core of moral autonomy and self-respect.

No human activity, however banal and routine, is considered unworthy of respectful consideration. If you are given a sandwich to eat, its presentation will gladden the eye and give pleasure to the palate, and it will be accompanied by a crease-free linen napkin. Those who have worked in the kitchen or the laundry to produce these civilized amenities will have attended to their jobs with dedication and pride in their handiwork. The commitment to excellence of all Opus Dei women — numeraries, supernumeraries, associates, and numerary assistants — in the performance of tasks from the most complex to the most trivial-seeming creates a low-tension, highly organized, and predictably calm environment in which the individual spirit may find both repose and uncluttered access to a heightened state of spiritual intention.

I attach great importance to the words "attended to." If there is one dominant quality I can ascribe to the women I

have met in Opus Dei, it is the extreme attentiveness —
a combination of sensitivity, discipline, and intellectual
alertness — they bring to every facet of their work and relationships. When you speak, you are heard and understood.
What you say is remembered. If a plan is suggested, it is fol-
lowed through. As the recipient of this attentiveness many
times over, I can say that the cumulative effect is to make
one feel more than appreciated as a human being; the word
I think most apt to describe what I feel is "cherished."

The other word I associate with Opus Dei is "serenity." Usually one associates serenity with contemplation
and withdrawal from the world. That is not the Opus Dei
way. Opus Dei is intensely engaged with our far-from-serene
world. In Opus Dei, serenity is the cumulative result of un-
shakable collective optimism applied to very hard work that
is made to seem effortless through rigorous attention to detail. All that is done is permeated with spiritual joy in the
performance of one's chosen duties. Taken together, the effect created is an almost palpable air of quiet uplift, and it
is a balm and an ointment to the world-battered soul of the
privileged visitor.

I am glad to have had this opportunity to reflect upon and
pay homage to the women of Opus Dei. I find that literally
all the persons in Opus Dei I have met seem a fascinating blend of confident self-possession and deep humility, a
combination unique in my social experience. I am grateful
to my friend Monique for introducing me to this rich world
of spiritual endeavor and practical achievement.

There is a half-congratulatory, half-hortatory expression
in Hebrew we offer during the synagogue service to a fellow
Jew who has made the ritual blessings over the Torah on be-
half of the congregation: *Yasher koach. Yasher* derives from

the word *ishur,* which means to sanction or approve. *Koach* means strength. It is my hope that the many worthy enterprises of Opus Dei will prosper, and the Work's numbers multiply. The need for what they provide with such lavish generosity of spirit is great, and the good they do is a blessing not only to Christians, but to all God's children. And so to all the members, but especially the women, of Opus Dei I say with wholehearted admiration: *Yasher koach* — May you go from strength to strength.

Introduction

As part of the Catholic Church, Opus Dei is dedicated to helping lay men and women throughout the world find and love God through their daily work and social interactions, and to spread the Christian message in and through their daily lives. St. Josemaría Escrivá, who was declared a saint by the late Pope John Paul II in October 2002, founded Opus Dei in Spain in 1928. Opus Dei is Latin for "Work of God." In some English-speaking countries, Opus Dei is often referred to as simply "the Work."

Interest in Opus Dei peaked in recent years when the author of a runaway bestseller, *The Da Vinci Code,* chose to cast an erroneous and distorted caricature of Opus Dei as the villain organization for his plot. This led to unprecedented media attention on Opus Dei, especially in the United States. Several misconceptions about Opus Dei remain widespread, one of them being the status of women within the organization. For example, the book claimed that women in Opus Dei are "forced to clean the men's residence halls for no pay" and in general are accorded lower status than men within the organization. And suspicions about the Work go far beyond the plot of the bestseller. Others have called into question, even labeled as backward, the fact that Opus Dei's programs are not co-ed, that is, the spiritual and educational programs, while identical in content, are carried out in single-sex fashion.

The reality is that Opus Dei's founder, St. Josemaría, taught that holiness is for everyone, that women and men are of equal dignity, and that women should use their talents to contribute to the Church and society.

This book lets members of Opus Dei speak for themselves in an effort to help the public better understand what a vocation to Opus Dei, especially for a woman, really means. The sampling of essays, interviews, and profiles of women in Opus Dei contained in this book may also allow readers to better grasp how an ongoing relationship with God helps people find deeper meaning and transcendence in the midst of their daily work — something that millions of Americans of diverse spiritual backgrounds hunger for. Opus Dei exists to help people achieve an ongoing relationship with God.

The chapters within offer a diverse mix of single and married women from various professional, ethnic, racial, and socioeconomic backgrounds. As in life, each woman is unique, with her own work, personal circumstances, and relationships. What these women share in common is that their vocation to Opus Dei adds a deeper Catholic vision and meaning to their everyday life, one that specifically relates to how they carry out their work and live as Christians in their varied circumstances, among their family, colleagues, and friends.

The profoundly secular nature of Opus Dei (that is, being in and of the world) can sometimes be challenging for people — especially the secular media — to understand. Typical media stories that have religion as a focus tend to want to show images of people in churches, in a posture of praying, surrounded by religious paraphernalia of some sort. This selective coverage tends to create a narrow perception of devout persons as always bound to those visual props. St. Josemaría described a similar bent that occurs in how people tend to understand the Catholic Church in general:

> The term "Church" is frequently used in a clerical sense as meaning "proper to the clergy or the Church hierarchy." And therefore many people understand participation in the life of the Church simply, or at least principally, as helping in the parish, cooperating in associations which have a mandate from the hierarchy, taking an active part in the liturgy and so on.
>
> Such people forget in practice, though they may claim it in theory, that the Church comprises all the People of God. All Christians go to make up the Church. Therefore the Church is present wherever there is a Christian who strives to live in the name of Christ.*

The calling to Opus Dei means for a person to be a member of society, to find and love God where one lives and works. Members of Opus Dei are no different from others in society, nor do they want to be different. They therefore have no need or desire to differentiate themselves by wearing a specific garb or congregating in a specific place of worship, or by surrounding themselves with religious objects. As lay persons among others in society, they try to bring family, friends, and colleagues closer to God through their personal dedication, example, friendship, and prayer.

In many ways, members of Opus Dei try to model themselves on how the early Christians lived and worked. They do try to attend Mass (the highest form of Christian prayer

---

*St. Josemaría Escrivá, *Conversations* (New York: Scepter Publishers, 2008), no. 112. Complete bibliographical data on the works of St. Josemaría Escrivá can be found at *www.Escrivaworks.org*.

for believing Catholics) every day, usually at their local parish, and they spend time in prayer (wherever and whenever is convenient for them), but they usually do this in a discreet way. In their verbal agreement with Opus Dei — which requires annual renewal for most persons in Opus Dei — they commit themselves to take advantage of the spiritual, theological, and philosophical supports Opus Dei offers to help them live all the Christian virtues and to live in the loving presence of God each day.

At the time of this book's publication, there are approximately eighty-eight thousand members of Opus Dei all over the world, with more than three thousand members in the United States. In both the United States and worldwide more than half of Opus Dei's members are women.

While all members of Opus Dei share the same vocation, each person lives it out differently. The majority of the members of the Work are married or called to marriage. These members are called supernumeraries. They live their vocation to Opus Dei wherever they are — in the midst of their families and communities. A smaller number of members are called to live a life of apostolic celibacy to love God with their whole heart to be available for the needs of Opus Dei worldwide. Without any change in their lay condition, their professional situation, or their position within the Church and society, they receive special training so that they can serve the other members by providing spiritual guidance and teaching the truths of the Catholic faith and the spirit of Opus Dei. Called numeraries, numerary assistants, or associates, they make up about 30 percent of Opus Dei's total membership. About 2 percent of the members of Opus Dei are priests, 1,956 priests worldwide. They are secular priests; they do not belong to a religious order but rather are drawn from the numerary and associate male members of Opus Dei.

Hundreds of thousands of women and men not in Opus Dei regularly attend Opus Dei's programs. These people receive spiritual support, encouragement, and Christian instruction from Opus Dei, but do not have a vocation to Opus Dei. A number of these persons have an association to Opus Dei and are referred to as cooperators, some of whom are not Catholic and some not even Christian. Opus Dei was the first institution of the Catholic Church to offer such a relationship to non-Catholics and non-Christians. While not members of Opus Dei, cooperators support Opus Dei with a combination of their prayers, alms, and time. Usually, though not always, they participate in some type of Christian formation — classes and seminars on spiritual topics — offered by Opus Dei.

Along with the essays and profiles contained in this book, we also provide information about the defining characteristics of Opus Dei, the life of piety the members live, and the kind of ongoing classes they take to help readers grasp Opus Dei's distinctive Catholic approach to helping people love God in and through their ordinary daily activities.

ONE

Children of Their Father God

The Equality of Men and Women

To begin with, it must be clearly stated that the equal treatment and value of women and men is established in Opus Dei's statutes and all the formal documents describing Opus Dei. Women and men in Opus Dei share:

* *the same vocation** and the same plan of Christian formation**** (that is, ongoing group and individual formation, comparable in many ways to professional development programs, provided to the faithful of Opus Dei);

---

*Vocation: The term used to describe the calling one perceives to receive from God. Both the Old Testament and the New Testament are replete with examples of persons receiving callings to follow God. To several of the apostles Jesus said simply: "Follow me."

**Christian Formation: "The aim of all Christian education...is to train the believer in an adult faith that can make him a 'new creation,' capable of bearing witness in his surroundings to the Christian hope that inspires him," writes Pope Benedict XVI in his apostolic exhortation *Sacramentum Caritatis,* no. 64. Different types of Christian formation are offered throughout the Catholic Church in many and varied forms. In Opus Dei, most of the Christian formation consists of personal one-on-one spiritual advising sessions, circles, Bible studies, classes on Catholic teachings, morning or afternoon recollections, retreats, and conferences.

♦ *the same practices of piety*, the same Christian customs and warm, family outlook proper to Opus Dei;

♦ *the same expectations* that Opus Dei has for all its faithful. Each woman and man in Opus Dei is expected to: (1) strive to become saints by struggling each day to live their vocation to Opus Dei in his or her personal circumstances; and (2) to take advantage of the ongoing classes of instruction and supports provided to them by Opus Dei.

This equality is rooted in the Bible and stems directly from God's fatherhood. "God created man in his image; in the divine image he created him; male and female he created them" (Gen. 1:27). Jesus, especially in the Gospel of St. John, speaks clearly and beautifully about God as a loving Father. "For the Father himself loves you" (John 16:27). "Your Father knows what you need before you ask him" (Matt. 6:8). There are many more references made expressly by Jesus attesting to the Fatherhood of God.

This concept, known as divine filiation,* is the foundation of a vocation to Opus Dei and is derived from Catholicism's emphasis on God the Father as Creator and first person of the Blessed Trinity. In *Christ Is Passing By*, no. 64, St. Josemaría puts it this way:

Awareness that God is our Father brings joy to our conversion: it tells us that we are returning to our Father's

---

*Divine Filiation: This is a term that means being a child of God. St. Josemaría Escrivá espoused that all joy derived from a person's sense of his or her divine filiation, i.e., his or her sense of being a beloved child of God. For those who have a calling to Opus Dei, this sense also serves as the foundation for that vocation.

house. This divine filiation is the basis of the spirit of Opus Dei. All men are children of God. But a child can look upon his father in many ways. We must try to be children who realize that the Lord, by loving us as his children, has taken us into his house, in the middle of the world, to be members of his family, so that what is his is ours, and what is ours is his, and to develop that familiarity and confidence which prompts us to ask him, like children, for the moon!

A child of God treats the Lord as his Father. He is not obsequious and servile, he is not merely formal and well-mannered: he is completely sincere and trusting. Men do not scandalize God. He can put up with all our infidelities. Our Father in heaven pardons any offence when his child returns to him, when he repents and asks for pardon. The Lord is such a good Father that he anticipates our desire to be pardoned and comes forward to us, opening his arms laden with grace.*

Do I always work with the joy of one who knows he or she is a child of God? This is a question all members of Opus Dei try to reflect on at least once a week.

---

*Grace: "Our justification comes from the grace of God. Grace is favor, the free and undeserved help that God gives us to respond to his call to become children of God, adoptive sons, partakers of the divine nature and of eternal life" (*Catechism of the Catholic Church,* no. 1996). "Grace is a participation in the life of God. It introduces us into the intimacy of Trinitarian life: by Baptism the Christian participates in the grace of Christ, the Head of his Body. As an 'adopted son' he can henceforth call God 'Father,' in union with the only Son. He receives the life of the Spirit who breathes charity into him and who forms the Church" (*Catechism of the Catholic Church,* no. 1997).

Understanding and having a firm conviction that God is a loving Father is what allows Christians, and therefore persons in Opus Dei, to flourish in living their vocation. It is the source of joy as well as their source of interior peace and strength.

TWO

From Toxicity to Transcendence

St. Josemaría and Contemplation in the Workplace

Jenny Driver, M.D., is an Instructor of Medicine at Harvard Medical School and a numerary member of Opus Dei. She gave this presentation at a conference entitled "Passionately Loving the World" in Toronto, Canada, in January 2003. The conference was held to commemorate the centennial of the birth of St. Josemaría Escrivá, the founder of Opus Dei.

I am a physician, not an expert in theology or philosophy, and I never knew St. Josemaría personally. I do, however, consider myself an expert in one thing: stress. Like many of my colleagues, I am a connoisseur of stress. We have an ice cream shop in the United States called Baskin-Robbins. It has thirty-one flavors. If stress came in thirty-one flavors, I would have tasted each and every one of them. A recent poll listed medical internship as one of the top five most stressful jobs in the United States.

On July 1, the first day of internship, the only people in teaching hospitals more nervous than the new interns are the patients who know that they are being cared for by green recruits, fresh out of medical school. My first night on call I was awakened by a page from an anxious-sounding nurse who said, "Come quick. Mr. Jones's heart rate is in the 200s and I can't find his pulse." I sped off toward the unit, flipping through the little book that tells me what to do in emergencies, my heart rate rivaling that of Mr. Jones. Much to my embarrassment, I tripped on a wire and made the final leg of my journey on my stomach as if "sliding into home plate." I glanced at the EKG, then gave my first order as a physician. "Let's get ready to shock him." Much to my relief, my resident calmly walked in and shepherded me through the resuscitation.

That was the beginning of a love-hate relationship with my pager. On busy days my pager would go off forty to fifty times, calling me to emergencies or asking for sleeping pills or enemas. Occasionally we would receive a welcome message from a friend, like "Let's eat." We called that "friendly fire." Eating, sleeping, and other functions we had once considered vital became subject to the dictates of our pagers and the condition of our patients. During my internship year, it was routine to work 30-hour shifts and 120-hour workweeks in the intensive care unit, caring for the city's sickest patients on a few hours of sleep, or none. We worked fueled by caffeine, adrenaline, and the fear of making a mistake.

Within a few months of internship, the idealism with which interns initially embrace their role often gives way to a kind of cynicism. This is reflected in the slang commonly used in the hospital subculture. Patients who were very sick and not likely to leave the hospital soon became "rocks." One might ask an intern on the geriatrics service, "How big is your rock garden?" Getting a new patient from the emergency room during a night on call was called "taking a hit." We began to use "torture" analogies to describe our work. "I really got flogged with pages last night," or, "I was hit hard."

We helped each other work through experiences like having to tell a young mother that she was full of cancer or making an error that led to a patient's death. The emotional, physical, and existential stress took its toll on us. The changes in personality produced by this stress were described as "becoming toxic." It was an accepted part of the job, and we learned to overlook our colleagues' depression and irritability as "toxicity." Each one of us ultimately faced the questions, "Why am I doing this? What is the meaning of my patient's suffering? What is the value of my work?"

But there was no time to think about or answer these questions. Products of a contemplatively challenged society with few spiritual roots, the majority of us kept working and kept going, hoping that the angst brought on by our work would pass with time. My workplace was desperately in need of a soul. For me, that need was met by St. Josemaría's teaching about the possibility of contemplation in the midst of a frenetic work life, which helped me transform my work from an experience of sheer stress into a place where I can encounter God.

My experience of contemplation and an inner life began on a Himalayan peak in northern India, surrounded by Tibetan prayer flags, thin bits of cloth whipping in the wind, as if echoing the prayers of pilgrims before me who had climbed the mountain in search of peace and spiritual help. I added my brightly colored flags to the faded and tattered ones. I had left my home, my culture, and my religion behind and was spending my junior year abroad in India. A poster child for Generation X, I had been baptized Catholic but fell away from the Church in childhood despite the example of a very devout mother and a Catholic education. I was turned off by what I considered the "corruption of organized religion" and the materialism of my society.

When I went off to college I had a deep spiritual longing. I majored in -isms and Indian studies and longed to "escape" from the world and from the ordinary. In Existentialism 101 I was intrigued by Martin Heidegger's concept of "authentic existence," a state of "mindfulness of being" in contrast to the "forgetfulness of being" in which one surrenders to the everyday world and becomes lost in its concerns. I lived a double life: my spiritual interests were my own private quest and were not integrated with the reality of my social and school life.

I climbed the mountain because there, far away from the worries and stresses of the world, I felt peaceful. I was able to forget about the contradictions and inconsistencies of my own life. It was easy to have a spirituality that demanded nothing of me that I didn't want to give. I felt I had escaped the "world" and material things with all their negative influence on me. I had moments of light and inspiration. Once, when I was spending time in Dharamsala, in northern India, where the Dalai Lama lived in exile, I noticed that bells would ring at odd times. I wondered what they meant. I went up to an elderly Tibetan woman, and asked her what the bells were for. She smiled and laughed: "They are to remind you that it is *now*." At that time, I did not grasp the meaning of her words. It was only later, much later, through the words of St. Josemaría, that I came to understand them.

As soon as I returned from India, my Buddhist veneer wore off. Fighting with my brothers and full of complaints, I was really longing for my mountain. I had no way of integrating my "spirituality" with the reality of each day. It was about that time that my mother introduced me to some women in Opus Dei.

I was immediately fascinated by their ideal of being contemplatives in the midst of the world, something I thought to be a contradiction. I was moved by their obvious love for and intimacy with God, who was a *person* to them, someone loving and understanding. These women were busy professionals and threw themselves into their work, but somehow they had a depth and peace that helped them absorb the bumps in the road that seemed to throw me off-kilter. Through my friends in Opus Dei and the life and teaching of St. Josemaría, I came to a deeper understanding of the truths of the Catholic faith. I began to pray and came back to the sacraments.* I no longer needed a mountain retreat to feel close to God. I had discovered him in the center of my soul.

The quest to live with constant knowledge of God's presence and providence was the "authentic existence" I had been searching for. So much of my life had been spent living on a level of worry and stress, trying to be "in control" and railing against my limitations. Rarely living in or enjoying the present moment, I ruminated on the past or was concerned about the future, having unrealistic expectations like "saving" all of my patients, never making mistakes, or always "looking good" to others. I realize how little I listened to people, how my worries about work and the people I loved crowded my consciousness.

---

*Sacraments: "The sacraments, instituted by Christ and entrusted to the Church, are efficacious signs of grace perceptible to the senses. Through them divine life is bestowed upon us. There are seven sacraments: Baptism, Confirmation, Holy Eucharist, Penance, Anointing of the Sick, Holy Orders, and Matrimony" (*Compendium of the Catechism of the Catholic Church*, no. 224).

I began to understand the inner struggle that was needed in order to overcome the restlessness and anxiety that had characterized my life to that point and to understand the transforming power of the sense of being a child of God. God was no longer an impersonal spectator or harsh critic, but rather a loving parent, who was intimately involved in the happenings of each moment. St. Josemaría described this awareness of being a beloved child of God as divine filiation. It is the wellspring from which his whole spiritual life flowed.

So much of my "toxicity" stemmed from a lack of inner life and not knowing how to have balance in my life or expectations. In my opinion Martha was toxic when she complained to Jesus that Mary wasn't helping. It wasn't because Martha was working and Mary was loving. It was because Martha didn't see that work could be love. She had forgotten that God himself was close to her and that through her work she was serving him. She was thinking only of herself, and this is what led to her unhappiness.

As is described beautifully in John F. Coverdale's book *Uncommon Faith*, in a moment of incredible stress, when everything seemed to be going against him, St. Josemaría, riding in a streetcar, was suffused with a deep, profound, and permanent knowledge of, and confidence in, God's love for him. That confidence, that experience, of knowing that he was a beloved child of God was what allowed him to go forward. This was a life-transforming moment for St. Josemaría. It enabled him to have an incredible optimism and resilience in the face of disappointments, disasters, and betrayals of all kinds. His whole life is a testament to the power of one who knows how to become a child.

This power is beautifully illustrated by a vignette I read many years ago. It occurred during the terrible earthquake in Armenia that I'm sure many of you remember. A grade school had been leveled, and a large number of children were buried and presumed dead. There was no heavy machinery available to help remove the rubble. Long after the other parents had given up from exhaustion, one man doggedly continued digging for over twenty-four hours, until finally he heard the voice of his child. The little boy was saying, "Daddy, I *knew* you would come. I *knew* you would come." He just kept repeating that. It took a number of hours to actually extricate the child completely, and later relief workers marveled at that child's apparent lack of post-traumatic stress disorder, which many people have after a horrible experience like that. For the child, the experience had only confirmed the love of his father for him.

I remembered this story in the days following September 11, as I saw the toll that event had taken on my patients, who have cancer, and on their families. A young child is buried alive, but survives unscathed, while thousands of people are shaken to their core and require antidepressants or antianxiety medication, because of an event they witnessed on television. At its roots, anxiety is a fear of loss, a fear of rejection, a fear of meaninglessness. It comes from living without a sense of the providence of God, or from losing it.

St. Josemaría often repeated and meditated on the words *Omnia in bonum:* All things work together for the good of those who love God (see Rom. 8:28). He said, "My children, see God behind every event and circumstance." It has always interested me that the Chinese character for "crisis" is the same as the one for "opportunity." For St. Josemaría, accepting the events of each day as the will of God gave them a new meaning. Each "crisis" was now an opportunity for union with God and growth in virtue.

He used to say, "Don't say, 'That person bothers me.' Think, 'that person sanctifies me'" (*The Way*, 174). This simple advice has helped me see the difficult situations I encounter in my work as something positive, something God permits so I can grow in some way. This point of view gives my work a sense of meaning. It has even helped me be on better terms with my beeper. Instead of swearing every time it goes off, I have learned over time to think, "God is calling me."

In Christian terms, as I carry out my work for God, I am somehow participating in his plans to make the world, and myself, better. I begin to see the value of the mundane and the monotonous. I am able to have contemplative moments throughout my day. When I write prescriptions, I picture the face of the patient I am helping. When I sit down to do dictations, I offer that hour as a prayer for the patients whose stories I am telling. When I go to visit dying patients, I take their hand and comfort them in some way, and I become Veronica, wiping the face of Christ. As St. Josemaría would say, the ordinary happenings of my working day can "sanctify" me. In other words, I become less centered on myself and more on God and others.

Here is another quote I love: "I will never share the opinion — though I respect it — of those who separate prayer from active life, as if they were incompatible. We children of God have to be contemplatives: people who, in the midst of the din and the throng, know how to find silence of soul in a lasting conversation with our Lord, people who know how to look at him as they look at a Father, as they look at a friend, as they look at someone with whom they are madly in love" (*Forge,* 738).

I do battle with the things that separate me from God and lead me to anxiety and toxicity on many fronts. E-mail is an ever-present temptation, addiction, and vortex. I realized that it had become a source of anxiety for me and led me to interrupt my work and not work well. So I only check it twice a day. What a conquest! The daily struggle to put my work down when it's time to go is another thing I have learned, based on the inspiration of St. Josemaría. In that way my work doesn't dominate me.

There are many beautiful stories of how the spirit of Opus Dei has helped people find meaning in their work and do it for the love of God and others. One that has stuck with me particularly is about a friend, a member of Opus Dei, who runs a very large hotel in Houston. As you may know there is a huge medical center in Houston. People come from all over the world for treatment. My friend gives people who work in her hotel inspirational talks every week about their work, trying to inspire them to do their work well. One day, one of her employees, someone who made up the rooms, cleaned them and changed the sheets, said to her, "I just want to thank you, because ever since one of your talks when you told us about that priest and his work, every time I make a bed I think I'm helping the family of some small child who has leukemia and who is here for treatment. And I love my job now."

There is another story that has always stuck with me. When you work in a contemplative way, it has amazing effects on the people around you. This is a true story. It happened in a prison in mainland China. There was a political prisoner in solitary confinement, and he had only one little window he could look out of to try to connect with the outside world. Every day there was another prisoner who came and swept the courtyard outside of the window. It was the same man every day, and the way that man did his job saved the life of the man in confinement. It saved his sanity. Every day he would look out at the man as he swept. The man didn't do just a cursory job. He swept beautifully; if he missed a spot he went back and got it. And he worked with such a sense of purpose. That little thing allowed the man in solitary confinement to think, "There has to be a meaning in what I am going through, and I can make it to the end." This was a man without any specific faith. After they were both released from the prison, the man who had been in solitary confinement found out that the other man was a Catholic bishop who had been in prison for, I think, over twenty years. Every day, while he swept, he was offering his work to God.

But Christianity is not an *inoculation* against the daily struggle with our weaknesses, unexpected contradictions, friction with others, and fatigue. Christ himself faced and embraced the difficulties of being human. I have a lot of devotion to the stressed Jesus, the tired Jesus, the anxious Jesus. Jesus' public life was a lot like internship and residency. He was up all night and had no time to sleep or eat; he went from one patient to the next. Jesus showed his infinite wisdom by choosing to come to earth in the pre-beeper era, but people managed to find him even when he tried to hide. Jesus even got "toxic" to show us his humanity.

There is a beautiful scene where he is with the apostles. They are trying to cure someone, and they are just not making it. They can't cut it. There is a big scene, and they pull him in and ask, "Why can't we cure this man?" And the first thing Jesus does is look up to heaven and say, "O faithless and unbelieving generation. How long must I put up with you?" That has given me a lot of consolation and a lot of devotion to the humanity of Christ, who chose to experience the frustration we all experience every day.

How did he do it? Christ drew his strength from his rich inner life, nourished by prayer. He saw things with a supernatural vision and was spurred on by his mission, to redeem humanity out of love. He embraced every moment as full of meaning and saw it with the perspective of eternity.

Through my friends in Opus Dei, I discovered the joy and the adventure of developing an inner life. I began to dedicate time to prayer and draw strength from the sacraments. I began to see that my desk is my altar, the place I can sacrifice myself for others, the place I can encounter God. On a good day, I accept the double bookings, emergency calls at 5:00 p.m. on Friday, patients who arrive an hour late, and hours of disability forms as events permitted by God; on my bad days, my job is "flog" and I can get quite "toxic." Every day I start again.

In addition to bringing me closer to God, my work gives me the opportunity to reach out to others. I try to do this more by my example than by my words. As most of my patients have cancer, there are many opportunities to affirm their dignity and speak with them about their spiritual concerns. I'm sure you are familiar with the old adage that there are no atheists in foxholes. Well, I can tell you that there are very few atheists among those who are struggling with cancer. As a devout Catholic in an agnostic academic environment, I try to open the minds of my colleagues to the concept of a loving God and the possibility of an inner life. Through my profession as an oncologist and teacher

I try to help foster respect for the elderly and the dying. I sometimes find it hard to swim against the tide and have to ask for more courage.

There is a beautiful quote in an article by Cardinal Ratzinger [Pope Benedict XVI] written around the time of the canonization of St. Josemaría, in which he describes this sense of divine filiation and the effects that it can have for the individual person and for the world. He says, "Those who have this link with God, those who have this uninterrupted conversation with him, can dare to respond to challenges and are no longer afraid because those who are in God's hands always fall into God's hands. This is how fear disappears and courage is born to respond to the contemporary world."

I'm eternally grateful to St. Josemaría for helping me to realize that I didn't need to go to the top of the mountain in order to find God, and that I could find him in the center of my soul. I would like to end with these words of his: "My children, heaven and earth seem to merge on the horizon. But where they really meet is in your heart, when you sanctify your everyday lives."*

---

*St. Josemaría Escrivá, *Conversations* (New York: Scepter Publishers, 2008), no. 116.

THREE

Called to Seek Holiness Everywhere and at All Times

"Go, therefore, and make disciples of all nations, baptizing them in the name of the Father, the Son, and the Holy Spirit, teaching them to observe all that I have commanded you; and behold, I am with you all days, even unto the consummation of the world."

(Matt. 28:19)

"... Be perfect, just as your heavenly Father is perfect."

(Matt. 5:46)

"I am the way and the truth and the life." (John 14:6)

"Whoever wishes to come after me must deny himself, take up his cross, and follow me. For whoever wishes to save his life will lose it, but whoever loses his life for my sake will find it. What profit would there be for one to gain the whole world and forfeit his life? Or what can one give in exchange for his life? For the Son of Man will come with his angels in his Father's glory, and then he will repay everyone according to his conduct." (Matt. 16:24–28)

At the heart of its service to the Catholic Church, Opus Dei helps lay people keep Jesus Christ front and center every day in everything they do. How does this work on a practical level? Opus Dei offers a combination of resources, for example:

- a daily, flexible plan of prayer, especially geared for busy lay people
- weekly, monthly, and annual Catholic spiritual and theological development programs given by Opus Dei lay men and women as well as priests
- weekly and biweekly one-on-one personal guidance sessions by Opus Dei lay women and men, as well as priests
- Centers* and conference centers professionally conceived and owned by independent and local nonprofit boards, and managed as settings where members of Opus Dei and many others can find a Christian home environment to inspire and encourage them

The lay members of Opus Dei, as well as persons who attend programs without belonging to Opus Dei, remain members of the parishes and dioceses to which they belong. Opus Dei exists to serve the dioceses and parishes by

---

*Centers of Opus Dei: These are usually family houses or apartments located in areas where there are members of Opus Dei and cooperators who desire the Christian formation Opus Dei offers. A center of Opus Dei is opened after the local bishop has given his permission to the Prelature of Opus Dei to do so.

carrying out its specific mission: offering supplemental religious education programs and spiritual support to persons interested in finding and loving God through their ordinary work and social relations.

> "The objective is to make it possible for the faithful of the Prelature* — the cooperators** and the many thousands of people who approach Opus Dei — to have access to means to live their faith coherently in the world, to facilitate their encounter with Christ in professional, family and social activities."***

---

*Personal Prelature: "Since 1982, Opus Dei has been a personal prelature of the Catholic Church. Personal prelatures exist to carry out specific pastoral missions in the Church, and are part of the jurisdictional, hierarchical structure of the Church. Personal prelatures have a prelate, secular priests, and men and women lay faithful, united as a single organism to carry out the prelature's mission. In Opus Dei's case, this mission is to spread the ideal of holiness in the middle of the world" (*www.opusdei.org*, "Place in the Church" section).

**Cooperator: "Through their prayer, work or donations, Cooperators assist the educational and social undertakings promoted by the Prelature's faithful throughout the world. Besides Catholics, Opus Dei has Cooperators who are Orthodox, Protestants, or members of other Christian churches; Jews, Muslims, or followers of other religions; and people with no religion. One does not become a member of Opus Dei by becoming a Cooperator" (see *www.opusdei.org*, FAQ section).

***Marlies Kücking, international head of Opus Dei's women's programs, in an interview with Zenit.org in June 2005.

FOUR

"From Street Cleaners to Presidents of Universities"

Interview with the National Director of
Human Resources for Opus Dei's
Women's Programs in the United States

Born in St. Lucia, West Indies, as the youngest of seven children, Pat Anderson moved with her family to South Carolina at age thirteen. While a student at Duke University she first encountered Opus Dei in Spain. After living with a devout Catholic family for some months, she decided to convert to Catholicism and prolonged her stay in Spain, eventually discovering her vocation to Opus Dei. A few years later, she returned to the United States, completed her undergraduate degree at Wellesley College, earned a master's degree in Spanish from Boston College, and then taught for a few years in the Department of Romance Languages and Literatures at Harvard University. Some years later she went to study education and philosophy in Rome and, after that, worked with Opus Dei's international leadership team there. While in Rome, she was frequently called upon to serve as English translator for Bishop Álvaro del Portillo, the close collaborator of St. Josemaría and his immediate successor as head of Opus Dei.

Q: Give us a little history. How did Opus Dei come to be your life?

Pat: I grew up in a Methodist home and went to Catholic schools when I was growing up in the West Indies. My parents sent us to Catholic schools because they were the best ones around at the time. During those years, even though I was attracted to Catholicism, I never thought I would actually become a Catholic. Since I was a Spanish major at Duke, I decided to spend my junior year studying in Madrid. In the summer before classes started, I lived with a family for a few months and worked as their au pair. They were not members of Opus Dei, but cooperators of Opus Dei — that is, people who help and/or receive formation from Opus Dei. It was in that home that I really decided I wanted to become a Catholic. I saw clearly that that's what God wanted me to do.

Q: How did you come to Opus Dei?

Pat: I first heard about Opus Dei when I was in Madrid, from the mother of the family I lived with there. She realized that I wanted to meet Spanish girls my age in Madrid, so she put me in contact with a university residence of Opus Dei. I went, and that first day I really liked it a lot! There were young women my age who were fun to be with, and at the same time they took their faith seriously. They had social lives, went out, played tennis — which I wanted to do, but couldn't since I moved to Madrid — and I loved being with them. We would go to the mountains, play tennis, walk around Madrid, and at the same time I was impressed that they had this relationship with Christ. So I started attending activities at the residence, and at a given moment — actually the day I became a Catholic — I thought I was coming to the end of a road; my journey was completed. That day before the ceremony began, I was praying and reading *The Way* [a book by St. Josemaría]. I came across a point that said, that conversion is the matter of a moment, sanctification is the work of a lifetime. When I read that I thought, This is not the end at all! It is just the beginning for me! Honestly, it was kind of a shock, because I realized fully that there was much more to it than just becoming a Catholic that day. After that I kept attending activities, and also a few months later I became aware that it was for me, this was how I wanted to live my life, so I asked to join Opus Dei as a numerary.

Q: So here you were, you'd gone away for your junior year abroad, and you had become a Catholic. When did you tell your parents, and how did they react?

Pat: Well, I knew I'd have to tell my parents about my decision to become a Catholic, but I was a nervous wreck! I thought, They are going to come to Madrid and bodily take me home before I do such a thing. As a matter of fact, they had come to visit me in Spain earlier, and at one point I told my father that I was going to a Catholic Church. He said: "Don't let them hoodwink you. You stand your ground," and I told him: "Don't worry, nobody's going to hoodwink me." At that point I had no thought whatsoever of becoming Catholic.

The first thing I decided to do was to pray a novena to the Holy Spirit. After praying for nine days, I wrote them. I wrote each one separately. Basically, I told them this is what I think I should do, because I feel this is what God wants me to do.

My mother wrote me back and said: "I think it's wonderful; if your father says anything, tell me and I'll talk to him." And my dad wrote: "I wish you had consulted me before. But if you think this is what God wants of you, who am I to stand in your way?" It was such a big relief to get those two letters! That hurdle was taken away, and I went forward with my decision. I did stay on longer in Spain than I had originally planned — I had gone only for nine months and ended up staying for two and a half years! I did come back in between, however, so my parents did see me.

The first time I came back to see them in Columbia, South Carolina, I told them I was member of Opus Dei. They didn't understand what it meant, though I tried to explain it. Nevertheless, they could see that what I had done had made a positive change in me, so they realized that I was doing something good. They could see that I had benefited from it and had a deeper faith, and they were happy. Later, the first time they visited a center of Opus Dei, they met other members of Opus Dei, saw the environment of the house, and they were very, very happy — so much so that my father said to me, "I wish I could live in an environment like this where I could receive so much spiritual help." Both my parents were very spiritual people.

Q: When you see young people who feel they have the vocation, do you recommend they tell their parents that they're thinking about a possible vocation?

Pat: I do, yes.

Q: How does one go about telling her parents? For example, when should a young woman tell her parents? What is the point of view of the parent in that situation?

Pat: I think that it is important that there be openness with one's parents, even though each family is a little different. A lot does depend on your relationship with your parents. There should be openness with one's parents about life choices. I think it is important that parents know what their child is thinking of doing, even though many times children do things that parents have no idea about. Sometimes parents don't want to know! In any case, I think there should be openness, and I invite young people to be sincere with their parents so that they know what they're thinking.

Q: Speaking from your current role in Opus Dei, can you talk about the reactions of parents of the young women who have decided to become members of Opus Dei?

Pat: Well, the reactions vary. But I would say that on the whole, if the parents are men and women who have a prayer life, who have a relationship with God, it's easier for them to understand their child giving her life to God. If they don't have a close relationship with Christ, it can be difficult for them to understand wanting to give one's life, everything, to God. It's much harder for them to accept that. At the same time, you can find the parents who are not even Christian — they could be Buddhist or not have any religion at all — and they may have a child who becomes a Catholic and joins Opus Dei. Because they respect their child's ability to make those life choices, they respect that decision. So, definitely, it varies, and much depends on the parents and their relationship with their children, and their relationship with God as well.

Q: What happened to your life after your conversion, and then after joining Opus Dei later?

Pat: When I left Spain, I moved to Boston and completed my degree at Wellesley College. Then I went on to graduate school at Boston College and received a master's degree in Spanish. After Boston College, I taught Spanish at Harvard for two years, and was then offered the job as director of a center of Opus Dei in Massachusetts. I was there for four more years, and then I moved to Italy, to a town outside of Rome, where I studied for a master's degree in education and philosophy. At the end of my studies there I was asked to join the faculty, and I remained there for two more years. Next I moved into Rome, where I worked in the central headquarters of Opus Dei for the next four years.

Q: How is this studying related to Opus Dei?

Pat: If you want to transmit Christian theology and spirituality to other people effectively, you want to be as well prepared as you can be. Christian education and spiritual formation are ongoing for people in Opus Dei. In my case, I was involved in education before, and this was an opportunity for me to develop what I had learned in an international environment. So I did the master's program in education and worked on the faculty where I studied — which was a wonderful experience.

Q: Then what?

Pat: Then I worked at the international headquarters of Opus Dei in Rome for four years and came back to the United States in 1995, and I moved to New York.

Q: As you look back on your professional life, what are the highlights?

Pat: Teaching was definitely one of the highlights, because I love the classroom. Another highlight was working in Rome, because I was able to be at the source, as it were, and also to see Opus Dei developing in many different countries. That was wonderful.

Q: Is Opus Dei the same in every country?

Pat: It's different in different countries, and yet somehow still the same. In Opus Dei there are many characteristics that you will find here, in Japan, in the Netherlands, because it's one spirit and it has one message, and it plays out in the same way. But since the people are diverse, the setting is different, the national characteristics are singular: Opus Dei takes shape in different ways in different places. In 1993, for example, I spent some days working in the centers of Opus Dei in Kenya. It was a wonderful experience for me because, first of all, I had never been to sub-Saharan Africa before. There I saw how Opus Dei was not only helping people in their spiritual life, but also helping them raise the whole tone of their lives. We went to an area where there are tea plantations, and in order to help those people in that community break the cycle of poverty, members of Opus Dei were teaching the women and girls how to do crafts, knit, create and tend a small farm, how to grow bees and cultivate honey for sale. They were not only taught about their faith, but also literacy and trades, so that they could have small businesses at home and improve their standard of living.

Another thing that I found interesting was in 1994 and 1995 when I went to Poland. At that time there were only two Opus Dei centers in the country, in Warsaw and in Szczecin. Poland had come out of communism a few years before, so it was interesting to see how the Poles were reacting as they came in contact with Opus Dei. Before, their faith had been repressed under the Communist regime, and now they were very interested in strengthening it, developing their spiritual lives. Large numbers attended the activities and were grateful for what they were receiving.

Q: As you reflect back on thirty years in Opus Dei, has it been a good thing for you?

Pat: Absolutely! I would do it again in a heartbeat. My vocation to Opus Dei gives me a great deal of fulfillment. I feel that this is my life's work. Sometimes you find people, adults, who wonder what to do with their lives. I'm so happy to have known what my life's work was to be and to be able to carry it out.

Q: Have you never wanted a husband or a child?

Pat: Oh, certainly. I definitely wanted a husband and children, like any other nineteen-year-old, which was how old I was when I joined Opus Dei. I was dating and planned to marry. It's always good to remember, though, that when you're talking about a vocation, it is really God who calls you. And I realized that God was calling me to be a member of Opus Dei. I felt the call to follow Christ closely, without a husband and without children, and I have found it to be very fulfilling.

Q: So you didn't see it as a sacrifice?

Pat: It was a sacrifice, it is a sacrifice, but one that I make willingly and joyfully, because I get so much in return.

Q: What does Opus Dei actually offer its members?

Pat: Opus Dei offers many things in terms of spiritual guidance. First, Opus Dei transmits Catholic doctrine and Christian morals to its members and others interested in attending Opus Dei's programs. As part of the Catholic Church, members of Opus Dei try to be very faithful to the teachings of Catholicism. In our centers, for example, we offer spiritual activities such as retreats* and recollections.** We also offer conferences and workshops. All of this is aimed at strengthening one's prayer life because that's really what we are about. It helps us be better Christians so we can bring Christ wherever we are, and bring Christ to others. In addition to group activities, there's also individual guidance — in a sense, it's almost like having a personal trainer who helps us one-on-one with advice, guidance, in a tailor-made fashion, according to our personal needs and circumstances.

---

*Retreat: A period of intense prayer and reflection, ordinarily lasting between two and five days. In Opus Dei, retreats are usually silent.

**Morning, Afternoon, or Evening of Recollection: These sessions of prolonged prayer and reflection occur once a month and ordinarily last for two or three hours. They usually consist of several meditations given by a priest of Opus Dei and a talk by an Opus Dei lay person. Attendees typically have the opportunity of taking advantage of the sacrament of Reconciliation.

This builds up our prayer life, for our aim is to know Jesus Christ, so we can become identified with him. He becomes a part of our lives so that we can bring him to others — so we can evangelize.

Q: *When you think about how all of that translates into your daily life, what are the practices that you and other members of Opus Dei follow?*

Pat: In Opus Dei we live practices that have been and still are traditional in the Catholic Church. For example, we try to go to daily Mass and receive Communion. We also spend time in mental prayer every day. We read the Bible. We try to make our work something to offer to God — to transform work into prayer. Then there are other activities and practices, for example, every month we attend a recollection, that is, several hours devoted to reflection. Once a year we make a longer retreat of several days. That gives us an opportunity to stop and put our year in perspective and make goals for the next year. All of these activities help strengthen our relationship with Jesus Christ.

Q: *Where does confession* come in?*

Pat: We're encouraged to live all of the sacraments. And we go to confession on a regular basis.

---

*Sacrament of Reconciliation: "It is called the sacrament of Penance, the sacrament of Reconciliation, the sacrament of Forgiveness, the sacrament of Confession, and the sacrament of Conversion" (*Compendium of the Catechism of the Catholic Church,* no. 296). "Since the new life of grace received in Baptism does not abolish the weakness of human nature nor the inclination to sin (that is, concupiscence), Christ instituted this sacrament for the conversion of the baptized who have been separated from him by sin" (*Compendium of the Catechism of the Catholic Church,* no. 297).

Q: What about the rosary? I know St. Josemaría had particular affection for the rosary.

Pat: Well, love for the blessed Virgin is traditional in the Catholic Church. And the founder of Opus Dei wanted all of us to have a very strong love for the Mother of God, so the rosary is a part of our daily spiritual practices.

Q: If you reflect on Opus Dei as an organization and all the good and devout Catholics who are out there, is there such a thing as an ordinary devout Catholic?

Pat: I would say that in Opus Dei, we do try to be good Catholics. Opus Dei provides personal guidance and support on a regular basis to help us become devout Catholics. Certainly, people can become devout Catholics without Opus Dei, and I am sure many do. In Opus Dei, our calling involves seeking our own holiness in our daily lives, and we try to bring those around us — colleagues, family, friends — closer to Jesus Christ through offering up our work well done, through our example of struggling to be Christlike ourselves each day, through our prayers and sacrifices for them, through our friendship with those around us. John Paul II made an invitation to all Catholics to evangelize, and we are trying to do that on a regular basis in our daily lives.

Q: Is that the same as trying to get members for Opus Dei?

Pat: Our evangelical mission is, first of all, to do what St. Paul says, to be other Christs. We have to imitate Christ. If we want to imitate Christ, first we need to be men and women who are close to him and who bring him to others. We want to bring Christ to people and people to Christ. That said, most of the friends and the people for whom we pray likely will not have a calling to Opus Dei. When we offer our activities, we know that some people may be called, but not everybody is going to feel that call. It's a free and individual thing.

Q: *What is the role of women in Opus Dei? Is there truly fundamental equality?*

Pat: St. Josemaría had it very clearly in mind that men and women have a very basic and fundamental equality before God, before the Church, and in civil society. This was his message and vision from the very beginning of Opus Dei. Further, he wanted the women of Opus Dei — he spoke and wrote about this in the 1930s and '40s in Spain — to pursue and obtain the highest academic qualifications they could, as well as the highest level of professional competence they could attain in all professional fields. Men and women in Opus Dei are considered completely equal. The women of Opus Dei, for example, govern and direct their own centers and activities in Opus Dei.

St. Josemaría wanted women to be involved in any professional sphere they chose. Since he supported women in all their professional choices, he encouraged them to be the best they could be, because that way they could offer to God their best gift. He also wanted it to be very clear that the work in the home is a professional job as well — something that to this day is still not fully understood in our society. Many stay-at-home mothers often feel marginalized and undervalued by society. St. Josemaría was quite outspoken and progressive about the importance and professional dignity of this work. He empowered women who chose it to be their professional work, to do it in the best way possible, as he did in all the other spheres, including in journalism, medicine, politics, and economy. The same applied to the work of the home, because of its important role in society and in the fulfillment and happiness of everyone.

Q: When you look at the different members of Opus Dei, take us through the kinds of memberships, and what they are.

Pat: There's only one vocation in Opus Dei, and I think it's important for people to understand that clearly. Even though Opus Dei has around ninety thousand members, they're all called to the same thing, which is to follow Christ closely. They're called to seek holiness, and to evangelize, to bring others to Christ. This one vocation plays out in different ways because our circumstances are different, our commitments are different.

Q: How would you describe Opus Dei to a non-Catholic?

Pat: It's an organization that provides spiritual support and development programs. In some ways it's like a big international support group, and in other ways it's like a diverse international professional development organization. It welcomes people of all racial, ethnic, socioeconomic, and educational backgrounds. It helps people from all walks of life understand better the Catholic message that all are called to a life of union and intimacy with God.

Q: *Most people equate dedication to God or celibacy* with the religious life. How is a calling to Opus Dei different from a religious vocation?*

Pat: A religious vocation traditionally has involved: taking vows, being referred to as consecrated persons, and adopting a personal disposition known as *contemptus mundi,* that is, a renunciation of the world, so to speak. Often persons with religious vocations wear habits and in some ways are differentiated from other Catholics by virtue of their being consecrated persons. Some live in monasteries and convents. In Opus Dei we revere and admire persons with religious dedications. They provide important Christian witness and service to the Church. Occasionally, persons who attend Opus Dei activities discover they are called to a religious vocation. A vocation to Opus Dei, whether one is married or celibate, does not involve taking vows, being a consecrated person, or being separate or different from other lay people. Persons in Opus Dei do not "leave the world," but rather love and are called to transform the world by carrying their work with Christian love and a spirit of sacrifice. Religious by definition are not lay persons, and Opus Dei exists to help lay people find and love God in their work.

Q: *Is Opus Dei only for those who are highly educated?*

Pat: No, it is not. Nonetheless, St. Josemaría did understand and promote evangelizing intellectuals and highly educated

---

*Celibacy: A calling and gift from God whereby one forgoes marriage in order to completely dedicate himself or herself to God. The men and women in Opus Dei called to celibacy do not take vows of chastity, nor are they "consecrated" persons. See *Compendium of the Catechism of the Catholic Church,* no. 342.

individuals through personal and professional friendship. He believed that they especially need to hear and understand the message of Christ in order for the teachings of Christ to reach all corners of the world. He understood that the highly educated and persons in leadership positions had greater impact on society and other people. That said, Opus Dei is made up of an enormous cross-section of people, from street cleaners to presidents of universities.

Q: Opus Dei is frequently described as a highly "conservative" organization. . . .

Pat: People often confuse fidelity to the Church's teachings with political conservatism. People in Opus Dei are politically all over the map. Some are liberal, some are conservative, some are independent. Opus Dei does not involve itself in the political leanings of its members. People in Opus Dei do have in common that they agree with the teachings of the Magisterium of the Catholic Church. Thus it is fair to say that they do not believe in euthanasia, abortion, etc. But that does not necessarily make them politically conservative. They should not automatically be grouped into that camp.

Q: Thank you, Ms. Anderson, for answering these questions. Do you have anything else you would like to add?

Pat: I think Opus Dei offers the Catholic laity (men and women) and other Christians support and encouragement to find and love God in their work, family, and social life. Within the Catholic Church, Opus Dei is one way among many to help the faithful lead holy lives. Anyone interested in finding out more about Opus Dei should read the writings of St. Josemaría Escrivá. Much of his writing can be accessed on the Internet: *www.Escrivaworks.org.* People can also visit Opus Dei's home page to find out more information and where they can attend a retreat or recollection offered through a center of Opus Dei. Visit: *www.opusdei.org.*

THE BASIC STRUCTURE OF OPUS DEI

As part of the Catholic Church, Opus Dei embraces and cherishes all the Catholic Church teachings provided for her faithful, for example: the sacraments, teachings found in Sacred Scripture, Tradition, and the teachings of the Popes and Church Councils. There are many and diverse rites, orders, secular institutes, and institutions within the Catholic Church, each with its own charism. Opus Dei's defining characteristics include the following:

+ It helps men and women from all racial, ethnic, religious, and socioeconomic walks of life find and love God each day in their ordinary work and family and social relations.

+ It is international.

+ It is primarily composed of and governed by lay women and men. There is a small proportion of priests in Opus Dei who serve its faithful by preaching and teaching about matters relating to the Catholic faith and administering the sacraments.

+ It is a personal prelature of the Catholic Church, which means: (a) its jurisdiction relates to persons, not geographic areas; (b) it exists to fulfill a specific pastoral mission for the Church; and (c) it is under the direct jurisdiction of the pope.

FIVE

"I Want to Love God with All My Heart"

The Story of a Founder of the U.S. Hospice Movement

The late Josefina Magno, M.D., is widely regarded as one of the founders of the hospice movement in the United States. Hospice care gives patients with terminal illnesses and their families the support they need so that the patient can die comfortably and with dignity. In our day, hospice care is widely available, but when Dr. Magno arrived in the United States in 1969, it was nonexistent.

Dr. Magno devoted her life to making hospice care available for everyone in the United States, the Philippines, and around the world. Dr. Magno's personal struggle with cancer was what initially led her to spearhead the cause of helping people die with dignity. A brief overview of her life will shed light on the kind of person and professional she was.

Originally from the Philippines, Dr. Magno began her medical career in private practice in internal medicine. She later became involved in health and medical policy when she served as the special assistant to the chairman of the National Science Development Board and then as the assistant to the secretary of health in the Philippine government.

She then moved to the United States. Her husband had died of cancer eleven years after they were married, leaving her with seven children. She never remarried.

Not long after her arrival in the United States, Dr. Magno was diagnosed with breast cancer. After undergoing cancer treatments, she decided to retrain as an oncologist at Georgetown University Medical Center. During her retraining, she observed doctors doing all they could to cure cancer patients. She saw that the accepted medical treatment — often not a cure but rather a prolonging of life while the cancer remained — could bring unbearable suffering to patients.

This prompted her to ask her supervisor why treatment had to continue in the absence of hope. Dr. Magno said, "His answer was classic: 'It's easier to go on treating them than to say that there's nothing more we can do.'" She realized something besides applying aggressive treatment protocols needed to be done for dying patients. Hence, her mission to develop the hospice movement began.

Dr. Magno helped implement and oversee hospice programs at a variety of hospitals and locations, including the Henry Ford Hospital in Detroit and Georgetown University Medical Center. It was there that she developed the Georgetown University Pilot Project on Hospice Care with Blue Cross/Blue Shield. This project defined the role of insurance providers in the delivery of hospice care in the United States. The data resulting from this project ultimately led to reimbursement of hospice care by Medicare and private third-party carriers.

Dr. Magno founded and served on the board of directors of the Academy of Hospice Physicians. She was appointed the first executive director of the National Hospice Organization; during her tenure as executive director, the number of hospice programs in the United States grew from one hundred to almost fifteen hundred, located in every state in the country. She also served for several years as the president of the International Hospice Institute.

Why did Dr. Magno — who already had an extremely full, accomplished life and was well along in developing and spreading her hospice movement — join Opus Dei? In a May 18, 1992, letter to a *Newsweek* journalist, she describes what attracted her:

I myself joined Opus Dei only very recently. I have been very much involved in a leadership role in the Cursillo Movement both in my country, the Philippines, and during my stay in Washington, D.C., from 1970 to 1984. I also was involved with the Charismatic movement, both at the Catholic University and at Georgetown University, so I felt that I was doing "quite well" in terms of my spiritual life.

I had heard about Opus Dei even before I left the Philippines in 1969. It was not until 1982, when I met friends who were in Opus Dei, that I began to have a faint understanding of what Opus Dei was all about. It is simple: sanctification and apostolate. If I am a physician, this is the work that God gave to me, and it is in being a physician that I can sanctify myself and sanctify my work. Thus, in my profession, I can find holiness and grow in my love for God. Because God had commanded all of us to "tell the whole world and bring the world to God," then the apostolate comes in.

As I strive to be holy, I should try to help others come to know and love God also.

From my point of view as a physician, the concept appealed to me. This is the message that Monsignor Escrivá had been preaching all of his life. Opus Dei is a call to sanctity in the world right where we all are. It is a vocation to holiness to the work that we are all involved in. He believed that with all his heart, and he kept urging everyone to achieve that with the help of the Blessed Mother and St. Joseph.

. . . What Monsignor Escrivá accomplished for me is to simplify what the path to my personal sanctity is. I want to be holy and I want to love God with all my heart, and the vocation to Opus Dei helps me to try to do that. . . . I assure you that I am not a fanatic. I'm just a physician who is trying hard to be God's apostle so that more people will come to know him and to love him. That is the mandate he has given to each one of us, isn't it?

Dr. Magno, who passed away in 2003 at the age of eighty-three, did not work to create the U.S. hospice movement because of Opus Dei; rather, Opus Dei provided her with different forms of spiritual and doctrinal encouragement and support to love God and souls as she did her pioneering work.

Most persons in Opus Dei, women or men, have not had — and probably will not have — the expansive and tangible impact that Dr. Magno's work has had, touching the lives of millions of dying patients and their families. Nevertheless, Opus Dei teaches and encourages all women and men to strive every day to carry out the ordinary tasks in their work, social life, and family life with love, a supernatural outlook,* and belief in the constant presence, interest, and action of God in each person's daily life. Further, Opus Dei's programs help them come to understand that this way of living *will* have a positive spiritual impact on all souls, especially those persons with whom they somehow have contact.

---

*Supernatural Outlook: This means seeing life and all events as being guided by Divine Providence; understanding the events and circumstances of life with the eyes of faith.

SIX

How Opus Dei Serves People

The main activity of Opus Dei is offering its members, and other people, the spiritual means they need to live as good Christians in the midst of the world. It helps them to learn Christ's doctrine and the Church's teachings. Its spirit moves them to work well for the love of God and as a service to other men. In a word, it helps them to behave like genuine Christians: being loyal friends, respecting the legitimate freedom of others, and trying to make our world more just. . . . Joining the Work only implies an obligation to make an honest effort to seek holiness in and through one's job and to be more fully aware of the service to humanity that every Christian life should be.*

The main function of Opus Dei is to provide lay people with ongoing programs of Christian formation. The use of the word "formation" here implies, not merely passing on knowledge relating to truths of faith, but also imparting practical tips to help people learn how to improve

---

*St. Josemaría Escrivá, *Conversations* (New York: Scepter Publishers, 2008), no. 27. This is from an interview St. Josemaría had with Peter Forbarth of *Time* magazine on April 15, 1967.

themselves through that knowledge. Through its programs, Opus Dei focuses on five areas of Christian formation:

- *spiritual:* Christian piety

- *doctrinal:* Catholic teachings

- *apostolic:* evangelization

- *human:* Christian behavior and manners as a manifestation of charity toward others

- *professional:* ethics and good work habits

This formation is given in group settings and one on one. These ongoing one-on-one sessions, classes, courses, and spiritual activities of formation are essential for those who have a vocation to Opus Dei to thrive, and they are also made available to many other people interested in receiving this Christian formation. The main goal is to help people know, love, and serve God, and to help them feel responsible and able to share their Christian faith with those around them, mainly through their example and friendship.

"The truth will make you free" (John 8:32). St. Josemaría understood clearly that it is impossible to love what you do not know, and he also firmly believed that to continue striving for holiness over time, formation needed to be received regularly.

The idea is simple. Much like the way people commit themselves to a regular regimen at a gym or to instruction and practice in effort to become proficient in a musical instrument, people in Opus Dei commit themselves to live certain practices of piety daily — also known as a plan of life* — and to avail themselves of regular, ongoing practical classes and other spiritual helps such as retreats. These help them deepen their knowledge of God and the Catholic Church and also grow in their practice of all the Christian virtues.

---

*Plan of Life: The regular practices of prayer. For a person in Opus Dei they include: frequent reception of the sacraments, prayer, daily reading of the New Testament and some other spiritual book, and small sacrifices lived in solidarity with Christ's self-giving. These are practices common to all Catholics.

SEVEN

Dancing Hula in the Quest for Holiness

by a Stanford Graduate and Mother of Six

Jane Reckart is a wife and mother of six children. She studied engineering at Stanford University, where she converted to Catholicism and later joined Opus Dei as a supernumerary. Her husband is in Opus Dei, as is her eldest daughter, a graduate of Stanford.

Everything I know about Catholicism, I learned from members of Opus Dei. I was an engineering student at Stanford when I met the man who was to become my husband. He was in Opus Dei, but to my inexperienced eighteen-year-old eyes, unschooled in organized religion, he was just a very Catholic guy, and I didn't want to be shut out of what was obviously an important part of his life.

I took classes about Catholicism from a priest of Opus Dei in order to explore Catholicism and decide if it was a faith I could embrace. I remember leaving each class thinking, "This makes so much sense. I wonder why everyone isn't Catholic." In due course, I became a Catholic, but I found the classes to be so helpful that I continued taking them. By the time I graduated from college, I had become a supernumerary member of Opus Dei.

I valued the Work because of the rich Catholic doctrine it provided me, but what clinched the deal, what moved me from thinking "these guys teach pretty cool stuff" to "I want to be a part of this," was the founder's overriding love of freedom. There is a story about St. Josemaría that I have heard several times, although each time it has been slightly different. This is my favorite version:

St. Josemaría once described a vocation to Opus Dei as like being on a path. It is one path, leading to God, but how each of us chooses to travel that path is indeed a choice, a free choice. We can walk straight ahead, zigzag a bit, do cartwheels, dance the rumba, or ride a motorcycle. We are perfectly free to live the spirit of Opus Dei in the way that fits our own individual circumstances.

That appealed to me because throughout life I never felt that I totally "fit" anywhere. The American dream, indeed, the American way of life, seemed to be designed for someone else, someone who didn't fit my description.

My parents were immigrants to the United States, so we had the whole first-generation thing going on: they had accents; we ate different foods; what we did eat, we ate differently because we held the knife and fork differently from everyone else. I even had dual citizenship with the United States and Great Britain because when I was born, my father was not yet a U.S. citizen.

Not only did I not fit in nationality-wise; I didn't even fit in racially. Ethnically, I was consigned to checking the "other" box when completing standardized forms, as my father is a Caucasian from England, and my mother is a cinnamon-skinned Jamaican. Nothing like checking "other" to make you feel different from everyone else.

While most American fathers were busy climbing the corporate ladder, my parents took a mildly hippie-ish tack, taking us with them to Micronesia, where my father was a Peace Corps staff doctor. I spent my childhood in the tropics, climbing guava trees and learning to swim in rivers, while my peers back home were tooling around on skateboards and roller skates. One has no need of those without paved roads, let alone sidewalks. While my stateside classmates spent their free time listening to the American Top 40, watching *The Brady Bunch,* and giggling on the phone, we had neither radio, TV, nor phone. When my father was needed at the hospital, an orderly was sent to our home to rap on the window to summon him.

Later, we moved to Hawaii, where we did have some American cultural necessities. We had a phone and TV, although the TV shows in Hawaii were broadcast a week later than they were on the mainland, so each year we watched Thanksgiving specials while in the throes of preparing for Christmas. Our town did have a movie theater, but it doubled as a storage center for coffins, so no one ever sat in the first few rows. Furthermore, with Hawaii's strong Asian population, the usual fare was kung fu movies. While on the other side of the Pacific, girls my age were taking ballet to increase their poise and grace, I danced hula, learned ancient Hawaiian chants, and made fragrant leis.

I went to college in California, after determining that I'd never survive more than an hour from the ocean. Even in college, however, I didn't really "fit." I was the only person I knew who came from a family of six children. To make it worse, my family wasn't Catholic or Mormon, so its large size didn't make sense to anyone. I can't tell you how many times I heard, "Why would anyone have so many kids if they didn't have to?"

Even after graduation, I still didn't "fit." While my class-mates went on to become executives, doctors, and lawyers who planned on having a child or two in the future, I became a stay-at-home mom to six children in rapid suc-cession. I even still dance hula on occasion. The pinnacle of my dancing career was probably the time I performed, three days before delivering our oldest son, for an especially appreciative audience.

What I learned from St. Josemaría's love of freedom is that it didn't matter that I didn't fit. I wasn't supposed to fit. God made me the way he did for a reason, and it is my role as a Christian to be open to his promptings so I can fulfill what he wants of me. I actually can't wait to find out how a Jamaican/English hula-dancing engineer with six kids fits into his plans. I know it won't be dull.

Opus Dei has enriched my life incredibly, both in a practi-cal sense and in a more spiritual sense. Practically speaking, and looking honestly at statistics on marriage in the United States, without the Work, I might not still be married to my husband, whom I love very much. St. Josemaría taught that one's husband is one's path to sanctity. With that in mind, I think I must be much holier now than I was before I met my husband — or at least, it feels that way some days. St. Josemaría taught us to love our husband's defects, and I love my husband's, even if some days I love them through clenched teeth. It helps to know that while I am clench-ing my teeth, he is also trying hard to love my defects, like the way I put the newspaper in the recycling before he has finished reading it, or the way I whiz through the kitchen and put away the milk, right after he has pulled it out in preparation to pour himself a glass.

Another practical consequence of my association with Opus Dei is that without the support of the Work, I wouldn't have all these children who fill my life to overflowing with love, tickles, and laughter. All my life I dreamed of having a large family, like the one in which I was raised, but I was caught unprepared for how debilitating pregnancy would be for me. I was sick, listless, and depressed for months with each pregnancy. I never would have had more than one or maybe two children if I hadn't learned from St. Josemaría that in generously welcoming children into our family, even when it is difficult, and in sharing with them the love God gives to us, we are building up society and sharing in God's work of creation.

Spiritually speaking, without changing what I do each day, whether it is scaling mountains of laundry or driving to volleyball practice or making yet another PB&J, Opus Dei has added new depth to everything I do. St. Josemaría taught us that our work is not an obstacle to spending time with God. On the contrary, our work can be prayer, when we do it well and offer it up to him. Thus, when I was scrubbing toothpaste off the blinds the other day (evidence of what I can only presume was someone chasing somebody with a loaded toothbrush), as long as I was doing it out of love for God and not focusing on what I'd do to those kids once I caught up with them, I was praying. Pretty amazing concept.

Offering work to Christ gives meaning to what I do. That's important, when what you do is change diaper upon diaper, interspersed with cleaning up spilled milk and policing interminable squabbles among siblings. There has to be more to life than just not strangling my kids. There is.

St. Josemaría taught us to embrace the cross, especially the little crosses that God sends our way each day. And I'll tell you, if finding an exploded pen in a dryer full of clothes — not once but three times in as many weeks — isn't a cross, then I don't know what is.

The Work provides me with a moral compass for the ethical decisions that crop up daily, like the weeds in my garden. I've been especially grateful for that compass when teaching our children how to apply Catholic morality to their hectic, very twenty-first-century lives. All parents have moral standards that they want to pass on to their children, but Opus Dei has helped me articulate those standards to my children and explain why they are important. Thus I can say, "Whacking your sister with a Power Ranger is not wrong because I said so, but because we all need to learn to control our anger, and in fact, isn't it wonderful that you have a sister who provides you with so many opportunities to control yours?" In addition, the Work has given me the confidence to stick with those moral standards, even when it seems like no one else does. That helps when the kids come home for the umpteenth time and plead, "Please may I have a Gameboy/Nintendo/electronic gadget of the moment? I am the only one in my class who doesn't have one." Instead of worrying that I might be mistaken, if indeed we are the only family in the greater Tucson area that does not own said toy, I can confidently, albeit wearily, explain that our time is a gift from God, so we should spend it well on homework, chores, or even conversing with our family.

I learned how to be a mother from my mom. I learned how to be a Catholic mother from my friends in the Work. I remember with gratitude one friend in particular, who was pregnant with her sixth child when I was pregnant with my first. She let me come over and go sledding with her kids — it was my first winter with snow. She also taught me that shopping for children's clothes at secondhand stores made absolute sense because kids outgrow their clothes before they wear them out. We still shop at secondhand stores, and the money we have saved on clothes has been put to more meaningful use. Christian poverty, as I learned it from St. Josemaría, lies in not filling your heart with things, but instead using material goods to fulfill God's plan, while being detached from them so your heart is available to love God. This has been indispensable when I discuss with my teens why they can't have name-brand jeans, or a car that's younger than they are.

I learned that God gave us our skills and talents for a reason, and we need to make them available to him to use in his great plan. I also learned that God didn't give me certain skills, and that too was for a reason.

Take cooking, for example. I am a horrendous cook, and to make matters worse, God so designed our digestive systems that I need to cook three times a day just to keep my family alive. I have had plenty of time to contemplate how God's plan could be advanced by my being a miserable cook, while scraping yet another inedible meal into the sink. First, it is helping me to be more humble. Humility is rather an ephemeral virtue and can be difficult to pin down and apply to our lives, not to mention the fact that sometimes, especially in matters of pride, I am a slow learner. So God gives me three opportunities each day to pray, "Cooking this meal really is beyond me and I don't want to do it, but with your help and out of love for my family, I will try again." Second, I have learned that I show my love for my family and for God through my work, even when it is work I find difficult. Third, my children have become more under-standing, seeing me struggle daily with my lack of culinary skills. They've learned not to say, "Yuck! This tastes disgusting!" Instead, they give me a hug and say, "Mom, thank you for working so hard on dinner, but this one really isn't my favorite."

Perhaps most fundamentally, Opus Dei has provided me with a coherent framework around which I have built every aspect of my life. At the simplest level, the daily rhythm of my life is punctuated by the norms of piety I learned from the Work. Going to daily Mass, doing mental prayer, reading a spiritual book, and saying the rosary are chances for me to reach up to God, give him a hug, and thank him for my husband, my children, and the many other blessings he gives me. But the concept of a framework for life reaches far beyond how I schedule my day. It extends to how I see my family, do my work, make daily moral decisions, and even to the high value I place on friendship. There is no corner of my life that hasn't benefited from my association with Opus Dei, and for that I will always be grateful.

EIGHT

Intellectual Humility

by a Professor of Chemistry and Biochemistry

I (Elizabeth Komives, Ph.D.) have to admit that the first time I met members of Opus Dei, two things struck me. First, these were really smart people who knew why they believed the teachings of the Catholic faith and could explain them. Second, these were hard-working people who saw their daily work as a service to humanity. Soon after starting to attend the classes in Catholic doctrine (mine was fairly rudimentary) and especially after working with women members of Opus Dei to put on a Leadership Camp for young girls, I began to sense that God might also be calling me to be a member of Opus Dei. One of the many awesome things about a call to Opus Dei is that God wants you to continue pursuing your professional work, whatever that may be, and to do it in his service. At the time, I was a junior in high school, but I already knew that I wanted to have a career in science. I thought I wanted to be a medical doctor. To serve God through your profession means to do it the best you can for his glory, and this coincided with my upbringing in which we were always expected to do our best.

Although I was from a small farming town in Wisconsin, I was encouraged by the members of Opus Dei to reach for the top, and everyone was happy for me when my acceptance to MIT arrived in the mail. Luckily, MIT is in Boston, where there is a student residence, Bayridge, where the spiritual formation is entrusted to Opus Dei. At first I thought I would live in the women's dorm, but that was until I spent a few nights there during Rush Week. I quickly realized that I didn't feel comfortable with the atmosphere of the dorm and requested that I be allowed to live "off-campus" at Bayridge Residence. After passing an interview process "to assess my maturity," I was allowed by the MIT administration to live at Bayridge. It was a great atmosphere and a well-needed balance to the rather nerdy atmosphere at MIT. The director of Bayridge taught me to have an open mind about other ways of doing things, when it was a matter of opinion. She taught me even to enjoy how people from some cultures can be so relaxed and do things more slowly than I was accustomed to. I had some difficult times at MIT, and I remember being so grateful for Father Sal Ferigle, then chaplain at Bayridge and a former physics professor. He had been through *everything* I was going through and always had encouraging words. While at Bayridge, I made a firm commitment to a vocation as an associate member of Opus Dei.

A woman numerary member who also lived at Bayridge at the time, Karen Schmidt, was sick with multiple sclerosis, and her condition was deteriorating, so I remember spending Saturdays at the side of her hospital bed reading to her, praying with her, and telling her about my friends at school. This experience made me realize that I did not want to be a doctor. I wanted to be a scientist who helps in the understanding of such diseases. I remember being amazed that no one at Bayridge tried to influence my decision not to become a doctor, although many of my friends at school did.

They thought that if I *could* become a doctor, then I *should* become a doctor because they could not see the element of service in a career as a science professor and researcher. This is another aspect of the spirit of Opus Dei that I have experienced: everyone is free to pursue the profession of her choice.

After graduating from MIT, I went west to San Francisco for graduate school at UCSF. The women members of Opus Dei had only just arrived in San Francisco four years earlier, in 1978, so there was *a lot* of work to be done. I remember being so excited when I met two fellow students in Mass on Sunday; I invited them to come with me to the college meditations.* The three or four women from UCSF were the only college students who attended the meditations during those years. We tried everything at UCSF to meet more students — medical ethics courses, international dinners, you name it. I am still in contact with many of the women I met during those years, and several now are also members of Opus Dei or cooperators.

Things went well in graduate school, and before long I was defending my thesis and heading back to Boston for a postdoctoral fellowship at Harvard. I remember informing my research advisor that I was going to be away from the lab for a week because I was helping to run a camp for inner-city kids in Roxbury (a pretty rough neighborhood in Boston). The next day, he came in with a baseball bat he wanted me to take in the car for protection and several bags of candy for the children. I was also able to interact with the

---

*Meditation: This is the term applied to a half-hour-long session of prayer led by a priest of Opus Dei, the purpose of which is to help the attendees learn to dialogue more freely on their own with God. It usually takes place in a chapel before the Blessed Sacrament.

Harvard pro-life club, helping them with publications and inviting speakers. I also remember having wonderful discussions with a lab mate who was pro-abortion. We wound up creating a list of principles we could both agree on, and we each took them to our respective groups on campus for approval. The Harvard pro-life club endorsed the principles, but the "pro-choice" club did not.

When the time came to apply for faculty positions, I put the whole process in the hands of God. Another postdoctoral fellow in the lab was applying at the same time, and he was much more together than I was, so it was a nerve-wracking experience. Coincidentally, that was the year that a major news magazine came out with the "blacklist" of all the chemistry departments that still had no women faculty, and because I was a woman coming from Harvard, I got seventeen interviews! It was definitely a miracle that I was able to be hired at the University of California San Diego, which is ranked among the top ten in my field.

Life as a junior faculty member is extremely challenging — even worse than life as an undergraduate at MIT. I started a project that required lots of new experimental approaches I was not familiar with, so progress was really slow. Junior faculty are given five years in which to "prove" themselves by getting papers published and obtaining federal grant support for their research. I was spending nearly one hundred hours per week at work. By year four I had only two papers published; my one and only grant had run out, and the application for renewal was rejected.

I remember talking with Father Raphael, another seasoned Opus Dei priest, and telling him that I didn't want to get tenure because I didn't want to work this hard the rest of my life. He asked me how many more years I had to go. When I said "one," he encouraged me to stick it out, saying that if I happened to get tenure, it would open up my options and that I wouldn't *have* to stay if I didn't want to. The director of the student residence in Los Angeles organized a trip to Mexico City to visit Our Lady of Guadalupe, and she invited me to come along as one of the leaders of the trip. This was a wonderful, thoughtful invitation for her to have made because I was able to put my tenure in Our Lady's hands and regain my peace in facing the uncertainty. These events show how, at the same time that the leaders in Opus Dei do not try to influence the professional lives of its members, they are ready to give the spiritual support members may need to achieve their professional goals.

A lot of people were praying for my tenure. The prayers worked, and whenever we were without another experimental avenue, a paper describing the experiment we needed would be published, or we would have an idea that would give us the clue we needed at that moment. I was able to publish another seven papers; remarkably, all the outside experts who were consulted gave me favorable reviews, and despite a few negative votes, I was granted tenure. I remember that I had a Mass to celebrate this event, and I invited all the families who had prayed. Some sixty people attended, and Father Felice, who was a biology professor before becoming a priest, told them how my tenure was a certifiable miracle.

At MIT and Harvard, I learned that scientists should be self-assured. The goal is to propose a novel theory and then to prove it is correct by experiment. Science is incredibly competitive, so you have to promote your own theories or someone else will take credit for them. In a research university, it is okay to be a good teacher, but only if you don't spend any time on it: all your time should be devoted to research. It is difficult to see how to be meek and humble of heart while at the same time self-promoting. It is also difficult to reconcile being heroically Christian, which should entail having a spirit of service toward the students (whom we are here to serve), and yet needing to spend most of our waking hours thinking about and doing science. St. Josemaría taught that humility is not incompatible with being the best; on the contrary, it is false humility to not achieve all that we are capable of. He also taught that every job, including cutting-edge research, is a service, and that we should take every opportunity to make each person feel the care and compassion that Christ would have given them. I have found that working in the world of cutting-edge scientific research provides many opportunities to practice and teach humility and a spirit of service.

St. Josemaría taught there is perfect harmony between man's intelligence and God's intelligence, and our goal as scientists with faith is to discover and understand better God's creation so as to work together with God to finish creation. I have never agreed with the widespread notion that science and faith are contradictory. If we take the approach that we are discovering God's creation, there can be no contradictions! Scientists also have to be very careful not to let their own egos get in the way of searching for the truth. In my mind, humility is the key to doing good science; yet this is not the paradigm under which most scientists work.

It was my postdoctoral advisor at Harvard who taught me this valuable lesson. One day he asked another student in the lab whether he had gotten the result they were both waiting for. The student answered that he had indeed gotten the result, but it wasn't the one my advisor wanted. My advisor responded dogmatically that he did not want any particular result, he simply wanted the truth. It is important to design experiments in order to probe the system deeply, not just to prove a favorite theory. When I was still an untenured assistant professor, we characterized the disulfide-bonding pattern of the 5th EGF-like domain from thrombomodulin. To our surprise, the active form did not have the expected disulfide-bonding pattern based on other EGF-like domains. I was lucky enough to have colleagues who were willing to support me in publishing this surprising result. It wasn't easy going against an accepted paradigm. Some five years after we made this discovery, an independent group confirmed it. The head scientist from that group telephoned me to say that although he was certain they were going to prove us wrong, he just had to tell me how surprised he was that we were actually right. In our case, we had nothing to prove: we were simply characterizing the bonding of the molecule, and we stumbled upon this result. It frightened me to think that if I had not had the humility to recognize the truth, I would have sent my student back to the lab to continue repeating the experiment, insisting he must have gotten it wrong.

Managing the competitive spirits in the lab and fostering collaboration, students experience the joy of contributing to the common good. I learned this from my advisors also: each student should have a task that he or she is responsible for and that helps the entire lab. St. Josemaría treated the young people who came to Opus Dei centers this way as well. Each one, no matter how new to the enterprise, was made to feel that his efforts were an important contribution to the success of the whole operation. When each one has responsibilities that others' work depends on, they will learn how to practice a spirit of service toward others. My experiences at Bayridge Residence helped me learn how to smooth over cultural differences and to help people understand one another. Students spend a lot of time together in the lab, and such an intense amount of contact with someone very different from themselves is a wonderful experience. They learn that there are many good ways to do things, and theirs is not the only way that works. They learn about other religions and cultures and how each fosters certain virtues that promote the common good.

St. Josemaría said that thinking of others is one of the best ways to avoid pride, which comes as a result of thinking about ourselves. I've noticed that in a lab that is not internally competitive, the older students help the younger ones study for exams and prepare their oral presentations. They help each other with their experiments, and teach one another new techniques. To foster this spirit further, I also try to organize charitable projects that students can work on together. In addition, the students in my lab serve as mentors and offer presentations to local middle schools and high schools. At Christmastime each year, some thirty students from the university, many of whom were graduate students in chemistry and biochemistry, stage a complete Posada (a Mexican tradition of re-enacting Mary and Joseph's search for a place to stay in Bethlehem before Jesus is born), including the traditional songs and piñatas. Many of these students are not Catholic, and this is their first experience in learning about the Christmas story. One student said to me afterward, "Now I understand why they always show the figures of Jesus, Mary, and Joseph in a *barn!*" Each person finds a way to help: some repair the donated toys, others dress the dolls or wrap the gifts. Some time ago, one of my students married another graduate student in the department. Because they were both students, they didn't have enough money for the wedding, so I volunteered the lab to prepare the flowers. We bought the flowers wholesale and spent two days working to make all the bouquets, corsages, and table arrangements. It was easy to store everything in the large cold room we normally use for our protein purifications. Since then, my lab has done the flowers for two other labmates, and it is always a very enjoyable service. The last happy couple even listed us in the wedding program!

Science is moving very fast these days, and everyone has too much to do. Still, it's important for the students to see that we put their needs before our own. Faculty are often faced with the choice to do something themselves, which would be faster and easier, or to let the student do it, which would be more educational. Often, because of a lack of humility and of concern for the education of the student, we decide to just do it ourselves. Again, St. Josemaría offers a tremendous example. He put less experienced people in charge of things that he knew much better how to do. He told them later that he did so for their education. For me, the struggle to wait while education happens is a key aspect of my struggle to sanctify science, and I often ask St. Josemaría for patience, knowing he probably struggled with this also — and became a saint as a result.

Finally, St. Josemaría often encouraged people to face the difficulties squarely and try to find Christian solutions to today's problems. Every scientist today faces uncertainty and frequent rejection. Even Nobel Prize winners sometimes get their papers rejected without peer review, and the grant review process is not much more reliable than a lottery. Nearly every paper we submit from my lab gets rejected the first time around. I try to help my students read the review carefully and, no matter how unfair they think it is, to find something we can learn from it. The person who completed the review is a scientific peer, so if he or she appears not to have understood what was described in the paper, it is probably because it was poorly explained. I always tell my students that they should be grateful for the reviewers' efforts and should try to improve as much as they can from the criticisms.

In summary, St. Josemaría taught that in every field it is possible to live all of the virtues heroically. Although humility doesn't seem to be a virtue that fits with a career in cutting-edge science, upon reflection one can see it's a crucially important virtue. Humble scientists have real confidence because they care only about what God thinks. They are not afraid to admit ignorance and are therefore more able to stay at the cutting edge. They work well with others and foster unity that promotes the common good. These abilities will become more and more essential as science becomes more interdisciplinary. Finally, encouraging a spirit of service and a cooperative atmosphere in the lab makes it possible, despite the frequent rejections, for science to be done in an atmosphere of peace and joy.

NINE

In the Presence of God

Interview with a Top Marketing Executive

Claire Huang is a well-respected, high-ranking marketing executive who has worked at companies such as Fidelity Investments, American Express Financial Advisors, Wise Foods, and the Häagen-Dazs Company.

Q: How did you find out about Opus Dei, and how long have you been attending programs sponsored by Opus Dei?

Claire: When I moved to Toronto, Canada, I felt the need to feed my spiritual life and wanted to attend a retreat. So a friend of mine who had moved to Pamplona, Spain, said, "Why don't you just call Opus Dei and see if they have any retreats?" So I called. I went on a retreat, and that was it.

Q: Have you always been a devout Catholic?

Claire: Well, I've been a regularly practicing Catholic. I don't know if I would say I was a devout Catholic at that time. I would go to Mass, but it was almost out of rote and blind faith. I didn't possess the deep understanding of the Catholic faith and the discovery and learning that I've experienced since attending regular spiritual programs run by Opus Dei.

Q: *How would you say the spirit of Opus Dei affects the way you carry out your daily work?*

Claire: First of all, I think that every moment of my work should be carried out in the presence of God. For example, I was in a meeting today praying that the Holy Spirit would inspire each one of us so that we would arrive at the right outcome for our customers, our business, and the people around the room — praying that whatever needed to happen would happen.

Q: *And how does Opus Dei help you do that?*

Claire: The guidance I receive gives me the consciousness to be aware of the good that I should be striving for each day through the different situations I find myself in.

Q: *And how does it give you the consciousness? I mean, practically speaking, what does it do for you?*

Claire: Three times a month, I attend a circle,* a series of classes that deal with human virtues and living Catholicism to its fullest. And I listen; I take notes; I pray about what was said in the class. Opus Dei encourages us to pray, encourages us to make the ordinary extraordinary, by supernaturalizing, offering our daily work — whether it's doing the laundry or meeting or deciding on multimillion-dollar decisions. Every single thing.

---

*Circle: This is a weekly class (monthly for cooperators) that addresses different topics to help attendees grow in their life of prayer and practice of Christian virtue. The class usually lasts for thirty to forty-five minutes, is conducted by a member of Opus Dei, and is both evangelical and practical in nature. Members of Opus Dei as well as hundreds of thousands of cooperators and young people all over the world take advantage of this ongoing Christian means of formation offered by Opus Dei.

Q: "Supernatural" — what does that mean?

Claire: Supernatural means that life is not just about the human. If you believe there is a God and that God watches over us and loves us and knows every move we make, every thought we have, then all the things that happen during any given day have more than just human meaning. All of these things have a supernatural dimension because God is watching over everything that we do. And so accepting and recognizing that everything somehow comes from God and growing in that understanding of life instead of ignoring it is part of what Opus Dei is all about. It's about realizing that every part of our ordinary life has a divine dimension and that God meets us and we meet God when we seek out those divine dimensions found in all the small circumstances of our daily life.

Opus Dei helps me understand that Catholicism is realizing that life is not just about the human; it is about thought and intention. Christ said that you have committed adultery if you even think about committing adultery with somebody. And so the objective is purity of thought, purity of intention, offering what you have to a greater good, and that's God, that's Christ. When you try to live your daily life like this, you find yourself thinking thoughts and taking actions that aspire to higher levels of goodness (that is, explicit union with God) than if you don't think of those things. Living life this way helps me to stay on track.

Q: How does the spirit of Opus Dei affect your daily life in the way you deal with the people with whom you work? How would you say the spirit of Opus Dei helps you

in your relationships, especially with your colleagues or others?

Claire: One of the biggest things that Opus Dei has taught me is that we're all part of the family of God. I treat other people based on that principle, that is, the people around me are children of God. This of course includes not only my wonderful family, but also people like my administrative assistant, all the people who work for me, my boss, my peers, whomever. I try to treat them as people who deserve respect, who deserve the truth even though some of it is tough to hear, who deserve my best effort at being the best person I can be.

Q: What do you think are the biggest challenges facing women in our society today?

Claire: I think it's balance of work and family, love of family versus feminism, true feminism. True feminism recognizes that women bring different qualities to the workplace than men. Women have a nurturing attitude and do things at work that are caring, but not sentimental; thoughtful, but not harsh. Women add warmth; that's why motherhood is such a beautiful thing. True feminism means being everything that a woman is good at, for example, being efficient, multitasking, etc. Women tend to be good at nurturing relationships. They're great at many things while men bring other gifts to the workplace.

Q: What other challenges face women in society today?

Claire: Some people think that being feminine, nurturing, and family-oriented are diametrically opposed to being efficient, professional, and even ambitious. They think that the mommy track is the mommy track, and you're never going to achieve anything if you're on that track. Well I have a ton of women who work for me, and I encourage them if they want to be a mother, whether they want to do that full-time or part-time.

Some of my employees spend one day at home; they do part-time work and they love that, and they like the flexibility of the time that they're able to spend at work. They have the balance of baby talk and adult talk and they like that. But I don't think that's a derailment of their career. I tell them that being at home with kids is like a full-time career. Bringing up a child and making this child a productive, loving person in the world is more important than developing a new ad campaign or doing a new strategy for any business in the world.

Q: *How do you find time to pray and meet all your demanding professional responsibilities?*

Claire: I try to maintain a very disciplined schedule. I have a clearly defined rhythm in my work life, and in order to grow, I believe I must have a similar rhythm and pace in my spiritual life.

Q: *What are some of the ethical issues as you see it in the world of marketing and advertising for the masses?*

Claire: My guiding principle is: start first with what is good for the customer, and it will eventually be good for the company. If you start with what is good for the company, it may not always be good for the customer. Customers are intelligent. They can see. It will become transparent to them if companies are truly looking after their best interests. And then, when the customer realizes that you're taking care of them, you will eventually benefit by their loyalty, by their repeat purchase, etc. That's what has worked for me all of my career, twenty-plus years.

I think that at the end of the day, any good marketer always does what is best for the customer. You hear about all these companies trying to push their products, trying to push insurance or certain stocks or whatever, and that's why they get into trouble. They get into trouble because they're pushing products as opposed to pushing what is good for the customer.

Q: *What are some of the qualities you would encourage young women to cultivate in order to be successful and honorable professionals?*

Claire: My first piece of advice is to learn the trade and work hard. Understand whatever it is, understand it really well, and learn from the folks who are at the top of their game.

Then I would encourage young women to make sure that they do not suppress any part of themselves. They should be cheerful at work; they should be themselves. Success is hard work, understanding your line of work, your business, delivering results and being cheerful in the process.

I think cheerfulness is important because then people want to deal with you, people want to collaborate with you. One of the questions I ask all the MBAs that come to interview for jobs, for senior vice-presidents, whatever jobs they want, is: how do they get along with their peers? How do they treat their leaders? How do they treat the people who work for them? And that is just as important as: Do they get results? Do they grow the business? Results and leadership are equally important.

The last piece of advice, I would say, is find a mentor, find a woman who can guide you, someone who you believe has that balance, has the balance of good professionalism, who wants to do well, who is ambitious, who is strong, who can give tough messages and still be kind and think of the person. We always need somebody to bounce things off of, especially when you're growing in the corporate world.

Q: How many years have you've been involved in Opus Dei activities?

Claire: I have been regularly attending spiritual programs offered by Opus Dei since 1989. Life is about doing good and being a good influence and smiling and cheering people up and helping the poor and educating inner-city kids. Life is about bigger things than just hitting P-and-L targets; that's good too, but life is bigger than that. And God wants us to be much more than whatever great thing we think of. In fact, according to St. Paul, we are called to be "other Christs" — a really high goal! God wants us to be ten times better than we imagine, but we have to listen — to be with him, to pray, and to respond to him. And Opus Dei has taught me that there's so much more fullness that we can give the world if only we live looking for God's will in everything we do.

TEN

One Way among Many in the Universal Call to Holiness

The Church ... is believed to be indefectibly holy. Indeed Christ, the Son of God, who with the Father and the Spirit is praised as "uniquely holy," loved the Church as His bride, delivering Himself up for her. He did this that He might sanctify her (Eph. 5:25–26). He united her to Himself as His own body and brought it to perfection by the gift of the Holy Spirit for God's glory. Therefore in the Church, everyone whether belonging to the hierarchy, or being cared for by it, is called to holiness, according to the saying of the Apostle: "For this is the will of God, your sanctification" (1 Thess. 4:3; cf. Eph. 1:4).

However, this holiness of the Church is unceasingly manifested, and must be manifested, in the fruits of grace which the Spirit produces in the faithful; it is expressed in many ways in individuals, who in their walk of life tend toward the perfection of charity, thus causing the edification of others; in a very special way this (holiness) appears in the practice of the counsels, customarily called "evangelical." This practice of the counsels, under the impulsion of the Holy Spirit, undertaken by many Christians, either privately or in a Church-approved condition or state of life, gives and must give in the world an outstanding witness and example of this same holiness.*

The universal call to holiness was a central theme and teaching proclaimed by the Second Vatican Council. It reminded the Catholic faithful that all persons within the Church, not just the clergy and religious, are called to be holy. The spiritual assistance offered by Opus Dei is one Catholic way among many to help people respond to this call. Of all the people who take advantage of the spiritual assistance Opus Dei provides, some may receive a vocation to Opus Dei.

Within a Catholic context, for many the term "vocation" can conjure up images of priests and religious (that is, nuns and monks). This helps explain why Opus Dei was considered radical when it was founded in 1928. At that time among Catholics, the idea of a lay person having a vocation, that is, a serious commitment and dedication to loving God without taking vows, joining an order, or living in a monastery was unheard of. St. Josemaría was thought of by some as outlandish for proposing such an idea. Forty years later, this concept — that all lay Christians are called to holiness in the midst of world — was confirmed by the teachings of the Second Vatican Council in the 1960s, echoing what St. Josemaría had been espousing since 1928.

---

*Vatican II, Dogmatic Constitution on the Church, *Lumen Gentium*, no. 39.

What is the vocation of the lay faithful? The lay faithful
have as their own vocation to seek the Kingdom of God
by illuminating and ordering temporal affairs according
to the plan of God. They carry out in this way their call
to holiness and to the apostolate, a call given to all the
baptized.*

Opus Dei makes no claim to being the only approach or
way to pursue this Christian ideal; rather it offers people *a
way* of seeking union with God through their ordinary work,
social relations, and family. Millions of people all over the
world have come in contact with Opus Dei programs since
it was founded in 1928. How have they found out about
Opus Dei programs?

Typically, an individual knows a person in Opus Dei
and through that friendship decides to attend Opus Dei
programs. Opus Dei usually promotes its programs in a
grassroots — that is, word-of-mouth, friend-to-friend —
way. That said, Opus Dei's website (*www.opusdei.org*) and
websites provided by centers of Opus Dei around the world
also provide information to anyone interested in learning
more about Opus Dei and its programs.

Many Catholics and non-Catholics attend Opus Dei
programs and never receive a vocation to Opus Dei. Sometimes, after attending Opus Dei programs for a while, a
person perceives that he or she is called by God to a religious order or to the priesthood. Typically, only a fraction
of the people who participate in Opus Dei activities feel
called by God to live the Christian vocation according to
and supported by the spirit of Opus Dei.

---

*Compendium of the Catechism of the Catholic Church, no. 188.

How is a vocation to Opus Dei different from simply taking advantage of what Opus Dei has to offer? After attending the Opus Dei programs for some time, a person expresses his or her interest in joining Opus Dei.

Then, over a period of a year and a half, he or she receives classes on what a vocation to Opus Dei entails as well as a thorough explanation of the basic teachings of the Catholic Church. Also during that time, he or she tries to live the daily Catholic practices of piety proper to Opus Dei. This is commonly referred to as the plan of life. He or she also commits to receiving classes and spiritual helps, also known as Christian formation, provided by Opus Dei. This commitment might be compared to how the member of a varsity team or a concert-level musician commits to the regular practice involved in his or her pursuits.

If after this initial period the person grasps the obligations and wants to make a firm commitment to continue striving for holiness according to the spirit of Opus Dei, at that point the person can be incorporated into Opus Dei through a verbal agreement with the Prelature.

For most members, this moral agreement is personally renewed each year. However, after five years, some members — primarily those who remain celibate as well as a few supernumerary members — can make a permanent commitment if they so wish.

People can freely choose not to renew their commitment or cease their commitment to Opus Dei at any time. St. Josemaría explained that this was so because people in Opus Dei should remain in Opus Dei only because they desire to, not because they have to.

ELEVEN

Making the Ordinary Extraordinary

Interview with a Wife, Mother of Four, and Business Owner

Mary Beth Burger is a forty-two-year-old supernumerary. She is a wife and mother of four. She is a physical therapist and owns an outpatient orthopedic physical therapy clinic in Virginia. Her oldest child, Christopher, was born blind and suffers from other handicaps, including a form of autism. She and her husband adopted their second-youngest child, who was born in Vietnam. Mary Beth joined Opus Dei in 1989. She explains how she came to know about Opus Dei:

My mother is a member of Opus Dei and has been for probably thirty-plus years. She and another friend of hers had a little seventh- and eighth-grade girls club. I was part of the girls club, and they would have different activities down at one of the centers of Opus Dei from time to time, so of course we went down there together and we did activities and crafts.

She chose not to attend many Opus Dei activities during her high school years because she was busy with other things and not interested. She recalls attending a retreat or two.

Her mother never pressured her to attend Opus Dei programs. As was part of her family ritual, she attended Mass every Sunday during high school. Once she got to college — she attended James Madison University — she became active in the campus ministry outreach program. She enjoyed giving of herself to others through this program. She began to feel a need for greater Eucharistic devotion so she started to attend daily Mass and found spiritual nourishment in the Eucharist.* She knew there was tremendous emphasis on the Eucharist as well as encouragement to give to others in the Christian formation programs Opus Dei offered, and this led her to start attending monthly evenings of recollection at a center of Opus Dei in Washington, D.C. At the same time, she remained active in the campus ministry outreach program.

When I got to college I decided I would go to an evening of recollection at a center of Opus Dei because I liked what I heard and wanted to go further in my faith. Before then, other than going to Mass on Sundays, I really did very little to practice my faith. I adopted a grandmother at a nursing home and would go to visit her once a week or once every other week. And I did that for three years. And I also went

---

*The Eucharist: "The Eucharist is the very sacrifice of the Body and Blood of the Lord Jesus which he instituted to perpetuate the sacrifice of the cross throughout the ages until his return in glory. Thus he entrusted to his Church this memorial of his death and Resurrection. It is a sign of unity, a bond of charity, a paschal banquet, in which Christ is consumed, the mind is filled with grace, and a pledge of future glory is given to us" (*Compendium of the Catechism of the Catholic Church*, no. 271). Holy Mass — or the celebration of the Eucharist — is the highest form of Christian prayer, and for many Catholics it constitutes the center and root of their life of prayer.

to a place where adults with cerebral palsy lived. Once a month we did an activity with them.

Mary Beth decided she had a vocation to Opus Dei after she completed physical therapy school. She explains how it happened.

I was approached and asked, "Do you think you might have a vocation?" And so I prayed about that, and then I realized that I did have a vocation to Opus Dei. Everything I read — all the writings of St. Josemaría — everything made sense to me and it gave meaning to everything else in my ordinary life. It gives me a sense of purpose for what I'm doing day-to-day.

What follows are some responses Mary Beth gave during an interview about her life and Opus Dei:

Q: *Are you the sole proprietor of your practice? What kind of physical therapy do you specialize in?*

Mary Beth: Yes, I am a sole proprietor. Outpatient ortho-pedics, that is, I treat patients who have back and neck problems, people who have been injured in automobile accidents, people who end up with back and neck problems from sitting behind computers all day long because they typically aren't sitting nice and tall. I treat people with shoulder problems or who have had shoulder surgeries or knee surgeries, people who have fallen on the ice fracturing their wrist.

Q: *Do you find it difficult balancing your work and family?*

Mary Beth: Yes, it's a challenge. I'm blessed because I have my mother-in-law in the office so she can keep an eye on things, keep a pulse on things when I'm not there, and if there are issues that come up, I can address them when needed. But sometimes it can be a challenge to juggle being a wife and a mom and owner of a practice.

Q: You mentioned earlier that Opus Dei's emphasis on Christ and the Eucharist attracted you. But what made it click for you? Can you explain concretely about the impact Opus Dei has on your day, how it gives it meaning?

Mary Beth: Well, my children are a little bit older now, but, for example, changing diapers: thinking that if you're doing it well, you're giving glory to God by changing a diaper. When I'm treating a patient, saying a prayer for that patient so I'm not just trying to help heal the body, but I'm looking at a person as a whole when I'm treating that person. Another example: when I am making dinner and I get frustrated with something, being able to offer that frustration up and knowing that there is fruitfulness or there is a purpose behind everything that doesn't go right. If you understand that you can offer that up; it just gives meaning and purpose to what you do.

Q: How does Opus Dei have an impact on your professional standards, your training, and the way you carry out your work, whether it's your work in the home or your physical therapy work?

Mary Beth: In order to give the most glory to God, you need to do whatever you're doing to the best of your ability — whether it is in the house trying to cook meals or have the house in order. I'm not the most organized person, but I try to do things the best I can and do them as well as I can.

I take a lot of continuing education classes because I want to be as up-to-date as possible, because I want to be able to help the patients physically the best I can because then I'm giving more glory to God by doing the best I can be doing.

It's trying to make whatever ordinary things you do extraordinary by supernaturalizing or offering to God whatever you're doing. You're trying to do them the best you can whether you're out with the kids and at the park, or at work, and trying to be as cheerful as possible.

In the morning, before they wake up and I'm doing my prayer, the first thing I pray for is patience and cheerfulness for when the kids wake up and everyone is calling at me at the same time: Mom and Mom and Mom . . . just trying to keep the cheerfulness and the patience. Also I pray to see humor in certain things so that I don't react with my Irish temper but try to react to things as best I can. When you know you are doing it for God, you're trying to do it the best you can.

Q: The plan of life in Opus Dei is demanding. It includes prayer every day. Most people do a half-hour in the morning, half-hour in the afternoon, daily Mass, a rosary, spiritual reading, other prayers. Is that hard? How do you fit it all in?

Mary Beth: Well, you have to have a nice schedule, and for me I get up earlier than the children get up. And at times that doesn't work, so you have to have a sporting spirit and smile. And if one of the kids happens to wake up when they're not supposed to be awake yet, you still do your prayer while you're doing whatever you're doing with them. And you just talk to our Lord when you're talking to them. But

I try to get up before they get up so I can do my prayer, and I also do my spiritual reading before they wake up because it's hard to find as much time during the day to fit that in, especially now that they're older and don't nap anymore.

Q: You invest a lot of time in mental prayer, doing your spiritual reading. What does this really do for you? What's the payoff?

Mary Beth: Well, it gives me focus for my day; it gives me balance. It helps keep everything I do through the day centered on God. When I don't do the different things such as prayer or my spiritual reading or the Angelus at noon, I lose that presence of God. There are days when God hasn't been up at the forefront, and those days are not as fulfilling and don't have as much meaning. I'm actually much happier when I do struggle to fit them in.

Q: So living your plan of prayer as suggested by Opus Dei makes you happier?

Mary Beth: It makes me a lot happier.

Q: And what about the impact on the people around you?

Mary Beth: It makes a big difference because when I have the presence of God, when my kids are up in the morning, if I've done my prayer and I'm in tune, I say okay, this is for you, Lord. I'm much happier, much more cheerful, and a much better mom to them. If something happens, instead of blowing up, I can turn it around and say, "Okay, it's all right. Don't worry about it." I react very differently and in a much better, positive manner as a mom if I keep that presence of God through the day.

In the office when things are behind schedule or some-thing's happened administratively that I have to deal with, if I stop and say, "Okay, Lord, there's a meaning, there's a purpose behind this," that changes the way I handle the situation and the way I react to the situation.

Also as a wife, trying to be the best wife I can, to be happy and cheerful when my husband comes home. It makes a dif-ference when I've kept that presence of God during the day. If it's a day that I'm keeping our Lord in mind, when Tom walks through the door I'm a much happier wife and greet my husband in a better way than if I am running around frantic or just not thinking of others.

Q: How do you think Opus Dei supports you as a woman? From what you say, some people might conclude, "Oh, she's always thinking of others and maybe that means she's a doormat and she's letting people walk all over her."

Mary Beth: No, actually Opus Dei reaffirms me. If Opus Dei looked down upon me as a woman, I wouldn't be practicing as a physical therapist as well as being a mom.

Q: So Opus Dei supports the fact that you are a working woman both at home and outside the home?

Mary Beth: Opus Dei gives you guidance to find meaning in what you do, but it doesn't tell you what to do. Women are not looked upon as lowly. Opus Dei helps you to be the type of woman that you're called to be, that you want to be for God.

Q: Do you ever talk to your patients about God?

Mary Beth: Yes, I do, actually. As a physical therapist I see patients two or three times a week and so I do get to know them. And depending upon the patient, just saying little things makes a big difference for them. I have one patient who is actually a very good friend of mine now. She was away from the faith, and had been away from the faith for thirty years, and we just started talking. We talked about that she was Catholic and we started talking about God. Through some of the conversations that we had, she actually came back to the faith, went to confession, and now goes to Mass almost every day. It made a big difference in her life. For others, especially Catholics, I just suggest that they offer their pain up to God, or I try to just mention in subtle ways how they can think of our Lord on the cross and try to unite their pain to his, or put a purpose to their pain by offering for someone in their family who was having a problem.

Q: And do they usually take it well when you give that advice?

Mary Beth: Yes. Well, I go on intuition as to whom I say what to. I don't say that to every Joe on the street that I'm seeing, so it all depends upon the person as to whether I think they can understand that or not. And so those that I typically talk to about suffering are patients who show the potential to understand.

Q: Do you pray about your patients? If so, how does that work?

Mary Beth: I try to. It depends upon the day. If it's a better day I do better with remembering to pray for certain people, and if it isn't then it doesn't always get done the way it should be, but then I try again. Each day is a new day.

Q: And has anyone ever been offended when you've talked to them about suffering or God in that way?

Mary Beth: No, actually they have not. I try to do it in a very nonoffensive and not-in-your-face way, and I don't talk with each patient about God because once again it depends upon the patient that I am seeing and what he or she can understand and my relationship with that person.

Q: You have one child with serious disabilities. Can you describe Christopher's disabilities?

Mary Beth: Christopher was born with microcephaly, that is, a smaller head, and he was born with severe cataracts and severe retinal damage. He is completely blind and doesn't even see light or dark. And he also has what's called Asperger's Syndrome, which is a high-functioning form of autism. When he was about two months old, we found out that he was blind. We didn't know how severe. And then when he was in kindergarten I realized, gosh there's something else going on. And so we started doing testing and found out that he had the Asperger's Syndrome in addition to his blindness. We also recently found out that Christopher has a learning disability.

Q: Was that difficult for you and your husband when you realized he was blind?

Mary Beth: Well, surprisingly, and probably because I had the support of Opus Dei, finding out that he was blind was not a big deal. I just thought, Okay, Lord, you've given me this special child with special needs, and I know with your help we will be okay. This is a little extra challenge you're sending our way. I know a lot of visually impaired people out there who, with the right help and the right resources, live a pretty decent and normal life.

I remember there was a person from the Virginia Department for the Visually Impaired who told me, "You seem to be doing pretty well handling that your son is blind." She was shocked at how well we were doing. And I said it was because I have faith and look at things supernaturally. I think that helped tremendously dealing with his disability.

Q: What do you mean supernaturally? What does that mean?

Mary Beth: That means taking everything on a human level and bringing it above nature, giving it a divine dimension. Instead of just saying, "Oh my gosh, this person's blind," or "What are we going to do?" you look at everything with God's plan.

God has a plan, and by offering and raising things up to God, you say, "Okay, Lord, this is what's going on," or "This is your will." God is there, and you try to be one with him in all that you do.

Q: Were you ever sad about it? Has it ever made you angry at God or question him that your son has these limitations in life?

Mary Beth: There are times when I see another boy running down the street, and I wonder what it would be like if Christopher could just be like him. So in that regard it's a cross, a challenge, because he can't do a lot that they do. But angry, no.

Q: *Does your son pray?*

Mary Beth: Yes, we have a time of prayer, especially at night. We pray during the meals. The children don't actually pray during the day, but they see the example of what I do. We say part of the rosary together. Some days that works well, and other days it doesn't work, to be completely honest. It all depends upon the day. It's a challenge with Christopher to get him to offer things up. When he gets frustrated, he says, "I don't want to offer that up!" But regular kids can act that way as well. It's a challenge to get him to understand the meaning and value of suffering.

Q: *So in general do you think being in Opus Dei has helped you as a mother, especially with a child who has a serious handicap?*

Mary Beth: It makes me see my son as a child of God. All of us are children of God, and all of us are special blessings. But it puts a whole other slant to it when you see Christopher, and I know that he's a special gift that God has given me, and having Opus Dei has helped me to look at that very positively. If I didn't have Opus Dei, I don't know if I would be as positive in my thoughts. I'd like to think I would be, but it has definitely helped me stay positive and strive to be a better mom.

Having the Asperger's, a learning disability, as well as blindness impacts Christopher a lot. Initially I thought, Okay, a blind child, you can help him to be independent. But when you have the Asperger's and a learning disability on top of the vision problem, it changes how independent Christopher may become as an adult. My job is to get Christopher to be the best person he can be, to grow in God's love and wisdom and to be the best he can be. But I take one day at a time with the grace of God and with the support and guidance of Opus Dei.

TWELVE

The Preeminence of the Christian Family

"Our God in his deepest mystery is not a solitary being, but a family, since God's inner life is paternity, filiation, and the essence of the family, which is love," said Pope John Paul II in describing the love between the persons of the Blessed Trinity as the root and origin of all family life* St. Josemaría believed that family life was of quintessential importance for souls to live out their Christian vocation.

As a small part of the Catholic Church, Opus Dei has from its start tried to be more like a large, loving, multicultural family than an international institution. This family love derives from the fact that we are all children of God through Baptism. The members of Opus Dei strive to create and live a culture of mutual affection, understanding, support, and encouragement through prayer and deeds. The family spirit is intended to nourish members with the unconditional love of God so that they in turn love and care for their own families better and love and serve those around them as other children of God. It is meant to augment the family life each member enjoys with his or her own respective family.

---

*Pope John Paul II, Homily, January 28, 1979.

This family environment is characteristic of Opus Dei. It is experienced and enjoyed not only by the members of Opus Dei, but by cooperators of Opus Dei, relatives of members of Opus Dei, and others who somehow have connections to persons in Opus Dei. As part of this family spirit, members pray regularly for each other, cooperators, their families, and many others. They also pray daily for the intentions of the Pope, the local bishops where they live, and the prelate* of Opus Dei.

The late Bishop Álvaro del Portillo, the immediate successor and closest collaborator of St. Josemaría, explained that much of the spiritual and material manifestation of the family spirit of Opus Dei stemmed from what St. Josemaría had experienced in his own family growing up. Bishop del Portillo described the early influence of St. Josemaría's mother, Dolores Escrivá, and his sister, Carmen Escrivá, in helping to materialize the spiritual family life St. Josemaría was trying to create in Opus Dei:

> They [Dolores and Carmen] transmitted the warmth that had characterized the domestic life of the Escrivá family to the supernatural family our founder was creating. We learned to recognize this in the good taste exemplified in so many small details, in the delicacy with which people treated each other, and in the way the material things in the house were cared for, which imply — and this is the most important thing — a constant concern for others in the spirit of service. . . . We

*Prelate: The priest, usually a bishop, elected by members of Opus Dei. His election is confirmed by the Roman Pontiff. He has ordinary power of jurisdiction over the clergy incardinated in the Prelature and the laity incorporated into it.

observed all this in the character of [St. Josemaría], and now we saw it confirmed in [Dolores Escrivá] and in [Carmen Escrivá]. We could not fail to treasure all this, and so, with spontaneous simplicity, family customs and traditions took root in us, which even today live on in all the centers of the Work: family portraits and photographs, which helped to make a house a home; a special dessert for someone's [birthday]; the affectionate and tasteful placing of flowers in front of an image of our Lady, or in some other appropriate place in the house. . . .

The family atmosphere that is so characteristic of Opus Dei comes basically, of course, from our founder. But if he succeeded in setting up such a lifestyle for our centers, it was not in virtue of his founding charisma alone, but also because of the way he himself had been brought up. It is only right to point out that his mother and sister helped him immensely.*

The daily life of the celibate and the married members of Opus Dei is like the life of most lay Christians. They have their professional work (whatever it might be), their social and family lives, their various hobbies and pastimes that they enjoy. What perhaps distinguishes the celibate members from the supernumerary members of Opus Dei is that they are more available to care for the centers, programs, and other members of Opus Dei.

Numeraries, numerary assistants, and associates remain single because (1) they receive a call from God to do so (it's considered a gift), and (2) for apostolic reasons, that is, to

---

*Alvaro del Portillo and Cesare Cavalleri, *Immersed in God* (New York: Scepter Publishers, 1996), 68.

commit themselves to supporting and staffing the myriad activities and spiritual formation programs Opus Dei offers its members and others.

They are responsible for organizing all the Opus Dei activities and programs, that is, classes of Christian doctrine, classes on spiritual asceticism, mornings and evenings of recollection, retreats, and a host of other activities like professional development, youth leadership, and home management programs. The supernumeraries help in this task as much as possible and are particularly responsible for the apostolic activities related to cooperators of Opus Dei.

Typically, the numeraries and numerary assistants live in centers of Opus Dei. The associate members usually reside with their families or on their own — wherever it works best according to their professional commitments.

Centers of Opus Dei are Christian homes, and their hospitality services are, whenever possible, entrusted to the women members of Opus Dei. In particular, depending on their number in a given city, numerary assistants carry out this responsibility. Numerary assistants are hospitality service professionals, or, put another way, they represent a celibate version of "stay-at-home" mothers who freely choose the work of the home as their professional work. From the beginning of Opus Dei, St. Josemaría understood and proclaimed the professional importance of this work, so often carried out by mothers. It is a work highly valued by all the members of Opus Dei.

The numerary assistants together with some numerary women are responsible for the smooth and professional operations of both the men's and women's centers where they carry out their work. They are well paid and receive generous benefit packages for their work, which include full health care benefits and at least a month's vacation time annually. This work is typically referred to as the administration of centers.

Whether in charge of overseeing a men's or a women's center or a conference center, they have their own separate and private area of work, and they carry out their job with no interference from residents at the centers or guests at the conference center. The men and women who receive their services do so with the utmost respect and refinement. Numerary assistants, like all members of Opus Dei, are encouraged to carry out their work with a professional outlook and a spirit of service, affection, and prayer, praying particularly for those who live in the places where they work. St. Josemaría described their work as the "apostolate of apostolates," because they exert their professional energies and creativity to ensure that the material (and in some ways spiritual) home life of the centers of Opus Dei is welcoming, clean, well run, cheerful, dignified, and attractive.

> When I think of Christian homes, I like to imagine them as being full of the light and joy that were in the home of the holy family. The message of Christmas is heard in all its forcefulness: "Glory to God in the highest, and on earth peace to men of good will." "And may the peace of Christ triumph in your hearts," writes the Apostle. It is a peace that comes from knowing that our Father God loves us, and that we are made one with Christ. It results from being under the protection of the Virgin, our Lady, and assisted by St. Joseph. This is the great light that illuminates our lives. In the midst of difficulties and of our own personal failings, it encourages us to keep up our effort. Every Christian

home should be a place of peace and serenity. In spite of the small frustrations of daily life, an atmosphere of profound and sincere affection should reign there together with a deep-rooted calm, which is the result of authentic faith that is put into practice.*

---

*St. Josemaría Escrivá, *Christ Is Passing By* (New York: Scepter Publishers, 1974), no. 22.

THIRTEEN

What God Wants Me to Do

Interview with a Cuban Refugee,
Harvard Graduate, Wife, Mother of Twelve,
and Executive Director of a
Crisis Pregnancy Center

*Mary Hamm was born on April 9, 1954, in Havana, Cuba.
She was the twelfth of fourteen children. Her father was involved in the underground resistance against Castro, which
culminated in the Bay of Pigs invasion. Sometime around
1960, her father was arrested because of his involvement
in the Bay of Pigs and was in prison for about six months.
Mary has traumatic memories of those times:*

I was four, five, and six during this period. The soldiers,
when they arrested him, came to the house, and we were
under house arrest. And they moved in with us, so we had
soldiers living with us during that time. And the Bay of Pigs
invasion that weekend was very traumatic. We could hear
the bombs dropping and we could hear the planes and it was
very scary.

Presumably President Kennedy had promised air cover
that didn't materialize. They backed down at the end and

did not give the resistance fighters air cover, so it was a massacre when the Cubans landed without any air support. The Nationals [Castro's forces] were able to shoot them on the beaches with no problem.

We lost friends, my parents did, that is. I was little so we were kind of shielded from some of that. And when we came to the United States my parents would never talk about it. It was like a taboo subject, because it was just too painful. Three of my sisters were also taken prisoner and they were seventeen, eighteen, and nineteen years old, so they were very young. That was as traumatic, if not more traumatic, than the arrest of my dad. My poor mom had to worry, but they were released pretty quickly. I think they were in prison for only a couple of weeks. But the men were in for quite a long time, and they were sent elsewhere. And I can remember my mom trying to locate my dad for weeks at a time just going from place to place because they didn't have jails for all of these people. They just pretty much rounded up anybody and everybody that they thought was in any way connected with the Counter-Revolution.

During this time, Mary's mother was left to care for the children and unsure about her husband's fate. It was a hard time for the family. Amid all the confusion and so many prisoners to manage, Mary's father was able to gain release from prison because he was in touch somehow with the British Embassy in Cuba and was going to give testimony about an English citizen who had been arrested under false pretenses and was in prison with him. In return for his testimony they were able to release him from jail, but the Cuban government did not officially release him; thus he needed to flee Cuba.

Once out of prison, without being able to see his family first, Mr. Suarez was helped to escape to the United States with false papers. Mary's mother was informed of her husband's release and subsequent escape to the United States and then had to organize the rest of the family's flight to the United States. Her family immigrated to the United States in 1960–61. The situation was difficult. The family was scattered to the winds and sent to live with different families, according to Mary, who was six years old at the time.

For a year after we first arrived here, I went to live with an American family. So I had an American family that became my sponsor family. And I lived on and off with them for the next couple of years while I started school here.

It was hard on the whole family. They were not allowed to bring anything out of Cuba, so they had to start all over in a new country with a lot of kids and no money. Mr. Suarez, who had been a successful engineer in Cuba, found himself working two and three jobs at once to make ends meet.

Luckily the Catholic schools back then were very open to receiving immigrant families. There weren't that many around at that time. And so we were always able to go to parochial schools and to Catholic high schools as scholarship students.

Mary knew no English when she first arrived in the United States. She learned quickly, though, and became a top student, ultimately getting accepted to Harvard University.

For college I was lucky enough to be part of the first wave of Affirmative Action when they were looking for Hispanic students. And I was approached by my school counselor, who said I should apply to Harvard. At that point I wanted to study education or interior design, and Harvard didn't offer either one as an undergraduate major. But they assured me that if I got a degree from Harvard, I could pretty much teach where I wanted. Since I did not have any money, that prospect was fantastic. It was a great education for me. I loved being at Harvard.

Mary first came in contact with Opus Dei during her junior year in high school. She describes it this way:

I started going to Opus Dei activities. It fit very much with what my parents had been teaching me at home, and it came at a very critical time in my life because in my high school there were lots of things going on that were very upsetting to me in terms of the way Mass was being celebrated and what we were learning in religion class about the divinity of Christ. There was just a lot of confusion in the late 1960s. And a lot of confusion about sexual ethics, but when I met Opus Dei, I finally found a place where I could get answers and learn how to research the answers according to what the Church was really teaching. And it gave me a lot of peace and security.

Opus Dei also encouraged her to pray:

The encouragement to go to daily Mass and to have mental prayer and to say the rosary, those were all things that my parents had done. I don't know that they noticed the difference in me, but certainly I noticed that there was a lot more structure and a lot more peace in the way I was living out my life. My brothers got involved at the same time, so it was kind of like a family thing. We were all trying to be more Christian and trying to be more helpful at home.

Mary decided to join Opus Dei as a supernumerary when she was a senior in high school. She spoke to her parents about it.

I told my parents from the first day that I considered it, and my mom — I'll never forget — said the future of the Church is in groups like Opus Dei. She was very supportive. She had seen how much it had helped me already the two years that I had been involved in high school, sorting out all the things that were going on in my school and trying to understand.

For the most part, Mary actually ran the family household, with some help from her brothers, and performed many of the household chores because her mother suffered from many illnesses. She recalls how a training program at one of Opus Dei's conference centers, Arnold Hall in Pembroke, Massachusetts, helped her develop a professional outlook as she cared for her family's home:

Being kids and not really having the time or the training to do the housekeeping, we did it in a very unprofessional way. I spent a summer working at Arnold Hall, and that really opened up my eyes to professionalism in the home and the whole idea that the home is really the domestic Church and the place where we should have good home life.

One thing about leaving Cuba was that because my parents didn't have money here, they were not as socially active as they had been in Cuba, so they were with us. When my dad wasn't at work, and when my mom wasn't, they were always with us, so this poverty made us closer to my parents. And we realized that family life — the time that we would spend with our parents and with each other just entertaining ourselves, playing family games and having very simple get-togethers as a family — was very valuable.

And in Opus Dei I learned that that was God's plan for the family, that family life shouldn't be going off and being involved in a million different activities that pull people out of the home all the time. And that people should want to come to your house, and that it should be an inviting place.

During her high school summers, besides attending the Arnold Hall training programs, she also cleaned homes to make money.

It was great because I made a fair amount of money, and I learned how to maintain a home because my ladies would teach me what I didn't already know. And then it allowed me to be home for my parents to cook dinner for my family, so it allowed me to combine work at home, and I was my own boss, which was nice.

I don't know if it was reading *The Way* or reading something of St. Josemaría and learning about cleaning the top of a cabinet or the top of a door where nobody sees. And yet God sees. And I would do that all the time when I would be cleaning the houses of these ladies, and I would try to think of extra things that they hadn't suggested, but that I saw that needed doing. And they would be so happy.

I remember one lady saying, "Wow, what did you do in my daughter's room that the floor is so shiny?" And I said, "Well I got some wax and I waxed it." It was a wood floor and it had to be waxed by hand. Things like that allowed me to take pride in housework and not to look at housework as something demeaning but rather something that can give glory to God.

When asked if she thought it was sexist that women usually end up being the ones doing the housework, Mary responded:

Well, I didn't see it that way. I felt that, yes, the work in the home generally falls to women over men. We're talking thousands of years of inculturation of this division of labor between men and women. It didn't used to be that way when people had home-based businesses or when they were working in agriculture — when people farmed. Everybody was working together.

But I think it's part of woman's genius that she has that attention to detail. My husband and my sons all participate. They're on the chore list for the dishes and they have to vacuum and they have to do the chores around the house, but rarely do I see them wanting to get involved in preparing special meals or things like that. I think it's something that women innately are called to that's part of nurturing.

We just enjoy it more, but somebody's got to do the work of the home. I just feel that it's such an important thing and that our society has erred when saying that anytime a woman is doing that, she's somehow not developing herself. I think that's baloney. I worked in an office and a lot of times it's glorified as being more valuable work, but it's basically the same repetition that you find in any kind of position in or out of the home.

In 1976, two days after graduating from Harvard, Mary married her high school sweetheart, Peter Hamm. A recent graduate from Princeton, he was to begin medical school in the fall, so they decided they wanted to have that summer together as newlyweds. They also decided that they wanted to have children right away, which might come as a surprise to many, given he was just starting medical school.

Mary worked as a medical secretary for their first year of marriage and then stopped teaching when she had their first child, Katherine. She then did work from home. She took in babysitting and did translations and other work until Peter graduated from medical school. Peter and Mary lived in New York for four years while Peter was in medical school, and then they moved to New Jersey while Peter did his residency in New York City.

During that time my vocation to Opus Dei was really critical because I didn't have any family in the city, so it was really my sisters in the Work who helped me through that very difficult time with Peter being gone a lot and very little money.

The family moved to Washington, D.C. in 1985. By the time Peter was ready to join a private practice, they already had six children and were expecting number seven. In 1987 she started teaching at Oakcrest School, an independent day school for girls grades six through twelve, and with an affiliation with Opus Dei.

I taught one course, the Social Teachings of the Church and Marriage, to seniors. And at that point I think I had like eight kids under the age of ten. But the school was only four minutes away, and I loved it. I loved a chance to get out a couple of days a week. I taught it with another teacher. So I taught only twice a week, and she taught the other three days, so it was an ideal part-time job, and it gave me a chance to be with the high school girls. I really enjoyed that stimulation. I did that for about three or four years until I had two more children, and then at that point I stayed home full-time for about the next ten years. I was always running clubs and camps for girls because I was heavy on the girls — at that point I had seven girls and three or four boys.

When our youngest was four — it was 1993 or 1994 — I was very involved in a couple of nonprofits, the National Institute of Womanhood and Centro Tepeyac [a crisis pregnancy center]. I was on the board of directors. My husband called that a double negative since I was not bringing in any income and I was paying babysitters. It was at a time when we were going to be faced with four in college at the same time. So financially we were going to be under a tight squeeze.

So he encouraged me to try to find a paying position. I was already on the board of Centro Tepeyac, where they really needed somebody to do fundraising and to help move it into a different location, sort of build up the program. So I proposed that they hire me for six months. I would try to raise $30,000, and that would bring me from January to June. Then if it worked, fine, we could talk about my coming back in the fall once the kids were back in school. It was a very natural fit.

Centro Tepeyac, in Silver Spring, Maryland, is a pregnancy center — crisis pregnancy center is the traditional phrase for this type of work. It is for pregnant women who don't have insurance, who may not be married, and who are considering abortion. And they need a pregnancy test. The free pregnancy test is usually the main reason they come to us, but they come for options counseling.

We also counsel for adoption and give classes on parenting and prenatal and postnatal care. Eventually we moved into abstinence counseling as well, working with young people on chastity issues.

It was hard the first few years. I was getting paid for 20 hours a week; I was probably putting in closer to 30 or 40. And the center went from seeing about 100 women a year to 400, 600, 800. Now we see about 2,000 women a year. Of those maybe 350 or so have positive pregnancy tests. A lot of the women we're seeing come after they have their babies, and they come in for postnatal class or parenting class, or they come in for prenatal classes after the pregnancy test.

When asked how her vocation to Opus Dei impacts her work, Mary responded:

Well, first of all, a crisis pregnancy center is like the trenches of life. You're dealing with life-and-death issues on a daily basis. The women come to you. They're pregnant. They're often immigrants, and pregnancy is a huge problem — but it comes on top of a whole bunch of other huge problems.

So one of the things that we've had to learn as counselors is that in one hour you're not going to solve all of these women's problems. Basically what you're there to do is to give them hope and give them a lifeline to God. And again one of the things you learn in Opus Dei is that today's troubles are enough for today and you have to tackle things one at a time. And you have to learn to connect people to God.

We have this phrase that we say to each other to remind ourselves: you can only sow seeds and you're not always there for the harvest. Opus Dei teaches us to live in the moment, to live with the spiritual presence of God, connecting with other people so that they can learn to pray. We often say to the women, "Let's pray together." And we teach them how to turn to God, and we connect them to the sacraments, knowing how important the sacraments have been for us.

We run to the Mass for strength and consolation; we run to the nearby church when we have really big problems and we pray in front of the Blessed Sacrament. And on the way home from the center you pray the rosary for that woman or that baby, so you're constantly weaving your prayer life into your work life.

Mary went on to explain that the pregnancy center has no association with Opus Dei.

The center has nothing to do with Opus Dei. The other counselors who are not in Opus Dei may or may not be using some of the same approaches. But because I'm the executive director, I'm always trying to teach them how to live that unity of life where everything you do, you're doing with the purpose of serving God and others.

Mary has been living out her vocation to Opus Dei for over thirty years now — attending daily Mass, praying the rosary, practicing the other daily acts of piety involved in the vocation. We asked her what she believes living a life of prayer does for a person. How is it helpful?

Well, my temperament is very much Bohemian. I did not have much structure growing up because basically we kids ran the home. The structure of praying at roughly the same time each day, of keeping a schedule, gave me wings because it allowed me to accomplish so much more.

People talk a lot about time management nowadays, and there are many courses on time management. Yet in Opus Dei I think I learned how to manage my time because when you take time out to pray, you are also reflecting on what you're doing. And so it forms the next part of your day.

The days when I skip prayer I can see the difference. I'm running around like a chicken with my head cut off trying to tick off my to-do list, but I haven't really prioritized or thought quietly about what's most important. I end up doing a lot of things that seem urgent, but aren't really important.

So the time of prayer, the rosary, the Mass take you out of the world for that little bit of time to reflect with God. What does he want you to do and what are the more important things to do? So you are not just led by whatever is happening around you, which is my tendency. I'm very much a Martha. I'm not a Mary. I'll do whatever. I remember one priest saying we have to learn to waste time with God. Learning to "waste time" with God, for me, was very critical.

And while you're doing it, sometimes maybe you think, oh my gosh, at the end of the day it looks like I've done so little because I didn't take time out to do these things. Maybe there are days when you fool yourself and you think, Well I'll skip Mass because I have this important meeting and I'll do this and I'll wait to say the rosary until I get in bed, and then of course you fall asleep. And then you look back on those days and you realize that you didn't get as much accomplished as you thought because you were looking at things from your perspective and not with God's grace.

Certainly for me that whole plan of life structure brought a lot of serenity because I knew I was doing what God wanted me to do, and that brings peace when you have to leave so many things undone on a given day. It gives me permission to take time out and reflect and be with our Lord, and this feeds the rest of the day.

When asked how she managed to fit all her acts of piety into her day raising twelve children and working part time besides, she answered:

I learned a long time ago that you can't compare yourself to others, and that's a big temptation, that is to say, She's only got five kids or she's got four kids or she's got twelve kids. First of all, I had incredibly easy pregnancies. My kids are very healthy, and they're very smart and athletic.

I also have a tremendous asset that a lot of women don't have: I have a husband who is so into his kids and is so into time management of his kids and his home that it does free me up. So I wouldn't advise what I do to anybody else, because it's right for me, but it may not be right for them. And I really believe that to him who much has been given much will be asked.

Mary's husband, who wanted a large family from the start, is not in Opus Dei, though some of his closest friends are. Asked if any of her children received vocations to Opus Dei, Mary replied:

My oldest was very close to Opus Dei. She went to circles in college, she's gone to Opus Dei retreats and she has done a lot of reading and meditation of the words of St. Jose-maría, so she's very close to Opus Dei, but she's joined a religious order.

One of her daughters is very involved in Communion and Liberation, an international Catholic movement. Some of her other children have participated in activities of Opus Dei.

FOURTEEN

Loving God and Serving Others

by a Hospitality Professional

Marianne Doherty, forty-three years old, met Opus Dei as a high school student when she worked at the Arnold Hall Conference Center in Pembroke, Massachusetts. The conference center hosts retreats, workshops, theology and philosophy courses, and other programs. The spiritual and doctrinal aspects of the programs are cared for by members of Opus Dei.

Q: How about sharing a little bit about your family?

Marianne: Well, we originally were from Quincy, Massachusetts, and then we moved down to Duxbury. I have two older brothers and two younger sisters. My dad's an electrician. My mom was a secretary. I did all my schooling at Duxbury until I went to college. I went to Trinity College in Washington, D.C., and then transferred to Lexington College in Chicago. Later I went to Johnson & Wales in Rhode Island.

Q: Explain how you met Opus Dei.

Marianne: A friend of mine who went to school with me asked me if I wanted a job, because she and her mom were working at Arnold Hall Conference Center; her mother was working in the dining room services.

At fourteen, I told her I was too young to work, and so she dropped the matter. Then the following year, when I was fifteen, another friend of mine, Marie, was also working at Arnold Hall. I thought the two of them were having so much fun, and I needed a job. So I applied, and I started working there. I think it was the summer between my sophomore and junior year of high school.

I worked there probably for a good year or year and a half before I even started to understand a little bit about what Opus Dei was. For me it was basically a job — washing dishes, doing the dining room service, and that was about it. I had a lot of friends there, but slowly I got interested in the spirituality behind Opus Dei and what actually happens at Arnold Hall.

Q: *So you were there a whole year and a half before you understood there was a spiritual dynamic to what was going on at Arnold Hall?*

Marianne: Yes, because as a sophomore or junior in high school, I was very shy. I wasn't the type who went around curiously asking questions. But one day, my brother was late picking me up, and one of the staff members at Arnold Hall sat down and asked me, "Do you understand what Opus Dei is?" And I said, "Hmm, no, not really."

So she explained, and I think that kind of sparked a little bit of an interest. The other high school kids were all attending circles, and classes given by the priest. And slowly they invited me and I started going regularly on Saturdays to a half-hour meditation given by a priest and to confession regularly — things that I really hadn't done before that.

I'm a Catholic. I attended CCD my whole life, but at the age of sixteen, I still didn't even know the Ten Commandments by memory or even what they really entailed. I think I was in a generation when the Church was experiencing a little bit of a confusion, and in CCD we learned a lot about love, and everything was love, but there was nothing about doctrine, Ten Commandments, different things like that, and those things started to interest me.

I think the thing that really got me interested was when Pope John Paul II came to the United States in 1979. All the girls from Arnold Hall were going to see the Pope. They invited me, and I said "no." I even had an invitation to see the Pope in Boston, and I declined it too because as a teenager, to go to a long Mass just wasn't something that appealed to me.

So all the girls said, "No, no, we're going to have a great time. We're going to Washington, D.C." So I joined them for the fun of the trip, and John Paul II won me over completely, as he did all the girls there.

Some of the girls weren't even Catholic. And as he left, everybody was very moved. Even though we didn't even really understand a lot of the things he was saying, I think just by how he was, his charisma, you knew there was something very special and very holy about him. And that led me to get more interested in my faith to see what this man had. He's the head of my Church, and I don't even know who he is. And I got more interested in him and my faith.

Q: *How did you feel your life was changing as you got to know Opus Dei better and got more involved in the activities?*

Marianne: I had a relationship with God that I never had before. I mean, I was brought up Catholic and yes, I prayed, but there was something very personal that I was learning — a very personal relationship between God and me. I received spiritual direction and went to confession regularly with a priest, and that helped me a lot. Because there are so many things as a teenager you hold inside, and you don't know who to speak to. And they're not even intimate things; it's just things that you don't know.

For example, I went on my first retreat when I was a junior in high school. And I was very upset after the retreat. The retreat was very good, but in my case, I didn't know enough about sin. At the end of the retreat I went home and spoke to my mother. She explained things to me and reassured me that I had not committed any mortal sins. I think she was surprised at my lack of formation and realized I had not learned everything in CCD. I didn't know what a mortal sin or a venial sin was. So all these things really caused turmoil in my soul, in my conscience, because all of a sudden I thought, I've been offending God in all these ways.

Since I didn't know the difference between a venial sin and a mortal sin, everything to me seemed serious. So of course, at the end of the retreat when I spoke to somebody about it, they said, "Oh, don't worry. This is the difference: these are faults; these are sins."

Being from New England, I would say that we were brought up with a Puritan mentality. There's good and evil.

My parents are of Irish descent, and we were brought up with the idea of fear of God. You do things because you love God, but more because you're afraid of punishment. Because of what I learned in Opus Dei, I do things because I love God. Not because I'm afraid that God's going to punish me, but because I'm afraid of offending God, like I would be afraid of hurting my parents. It's a whole different outlook on the love of God, which I was never really brought up with.

My senior year in high school, I participated in a training program at Arnold Hall, and I stayed there for most of the summer — working and living in the conference center with probably a dozen other girls. And I had such a great time, and I really enjoyed the work I was doing: taking care of the conference center and things like that.

Then I went to college and I continued going to a center of Opus Dei to receive formation. But at that point, there was something inside of me saying, "This could be for me; to join Opus Dei could be something for me."

And I talked about it in spiritual direction. In Opus Dei there's different types of members. And somebody asked me, "Would you be happy working in an administration," which is taking care of the centers of Opus Dei. And I thought about it and I thought, well, I really didn't grow up taking care of the home much, but I really saw the importance of the administration of the centers, really making the centers of Opus Dei into homes. They're not school dorms. There's a huge difference if you go into a center that has an administration. You really feel at home. So I did two years at Trinity College in Washington, where I studied business, math, and education. After completing two years at Trinity, I still felt God could be asking something of me so I decided to transfer to Lexington College to study hospitality management. Besides it being much cheaper to attend Lexington, I also figured that attending a less expensive school was a better option for me than to continue incurring more debt from student loans. After deciding to transfer to Lexington, I saw more clearly that God wanted me to join Opus Dei as a numerary assistant.

A numerary assistant is a member of Opus Dei who has a celibate vocation. She gives her whole life to God and to the mission of Opus Dei. A numerary assistant chooses for her profession taking care of the centers of Opus Dei, the domestic part of the centers — making the centers into homes. And it really is a free choice. Sometimes people think numerary assistants are those people who don't have the education or the intellect for carrying on some other profession. And in reality, numerary assistants could have any profession, but they see the need. They see the need of the mother and the family to make the center into a home, and they enjoy that type of work and so what they choose as their profession is to actually take care of all the household work in the centers and create that family atmosphere in the centers of Opus Dei.

I receive a salary and medical benefits. And I also choose, like the numerary members, that any extra salary that I have that I don't need for my own personal use, I give to Opus Dei to help carry on the apostolic work of Opus Dei.

Q: *Talk a little bit about your parents' reaction to your joining Opus Dei.*

Marianne: When I really got more interested, in the summer of my senior year of high school when I was attending that training program, they saw a difference in me. They saw how much I really loved being at Arnold Hall.

When I expressed interest when I was in college, at that point Opus Dei was still very new. It had not yet been made a personal prelature; this was done by Pope John Paul II in 1982. And so my parents did some research and they went to the parish priest. The parish priest didn't know much about Opus Dei, and so my parents were afraid that it was a cult. There are so many things going around. So out of love, they opposed it. They wanted me to wait.

I decided to join as a supernumerary, which meant that I could carry on life exactly as I had before. I was still hoping to become a numerary assistant. It was the not getting married that I think was really the part that my parents had a problem with, the idea that I would choose a celibate vocation. They thought I was too young for that, and that I hadn't lived life and things like that. So in that sense, I did wait to join as a numerary assistant, but I joined as a supernumerary so I could still receive formation and better my life, better my own understanding of Opus Dei.

My parents opposed my vocation for a couple of years. But when I was graduating from Lexington College, which is a school connected with Opus Dei, my parents came out for my graduation. They were completely won over by everything, especially the affection they received from the members of Opus Dei. They had never been close enough to Opus Dei to actually see it and really understand it. And that began a process of their learning to love Opus Dei.

At different points when my family went through hard times, I was always there, and they realized that not only had they not lost me, they had received the support of everybody in Opus Dei. They were completely won over by the affection.

Q: Do you clean both the men's and the women's residence halls?

Marianne: Yes.

Q: Why can't everyone just clean up after themselves? Why are the women in charge of this work?

Marianne: Well, they do to a certain degree. They do the best they can. But I'm sure if you had brothers you know there's a difference in the way a woman's hand is in something than when it's just left up to all men. Women have an instinct or a sixth sense about things. And it's in our nature. We want things to look beautiful. And I do get paid for this work. This is my profession. It's not like I'm just being subservient. I take great pride in the way I clean. But I also look at it as a mother. When a place is clean, there is a certain dignity to that home.

Q: So the men aren't supervising you in this?

Marianne: Oh, not at all. It's completely separate. We try not to cross paths at all, and this also facilitates the work.

We have our own organization. To have set times for the schedule helps a lot. I apply my knowledge and professional training; I follow a plan and have goals that I share with my colleagues.

We do the same thing for the women. I mean, this is our house, the center, so the men's and the women's houses, we take care of both of them. We work with the same professional mentality and preparation for our own centers. It's not just for the men.

Q: *And you received professional training for this work?*

Marianne: Yes. I went to Lexington College, which is the only all-women hospitality college in the U.S., and then after that I went on to Johnson & Wales University, where I studied culinary arts. I also frequently attend workshops and refresher courses.

Q: *Do you live the same spirit of penance as the other celibate members? Specifically do you practice corporal mortification?* *

Marianne: Yes. You have voluntary mortifications as well as involuntary, like everybody in life. Things come your way that are not easy, and you could say that's a mortification. But then there are things that you volunteer, that you voluntarily take upon yourself to offer as a sacrifice — like the whole idea of Lent. For forty days, all Catholics are encouraged to give up something to offer as a sacrifice, to take a little bit of the cross of Christ and share in that cross. In terms of my voluntary mortifications, the ones I freely choose to do myself, sure, I wear the cilice for two hours a day. And honestly, there are things that, like wearing a girdle, that are even worse than wearing a cilice. I think people

---

*Mortification: This is a term drawn from classical asceticism referring to the practice of self-denial and austerity for the sake of spiritual growth. It literally means to die to oneself. "Jesus said to his disciples, 'Whoever wishes to come after me must deny himself, take up his cross, and follow me. For whoever wishes to save his life will lose it, but whoever loses his life for my sake will find it'" (Matt. 16:19–20).

just build it up to be something that it's really not. It's a reminder in a small way of Christ's suffering for us, much like how Catholics do not eat red meat on Fridays in Lent.

Q: Well, why do you wear it?

Marianne: Because I feel it helps me to share in a little bit of that cross. I also feel that it helps me as a person to build a stronger character.

Look at society now. Everybody is so soft. And when some little problem comes along, people are overwhelmed by their big crisis. But for those people who have a constant struggle and overcome themselves, those things aren't any big deal. It's almost like a self-discipline.

But the real reason I wear it is so that I can share in a little bit of Christ's cross, because I feel my life is pretty easy. I look at my life and I compare myself to a mother of a large family, a mother who has little kids, who's on 24/7, up during the night feeding those children. There are many people who have a very rough life, and I feel personally that my life is not that difficult. And I could get very, very comfortable, and this is just one way of helping me with that, and also to look at the cross and offer the sacrifice for souls.

Q: What is your life like?

Marianne: Well, it's pretty busy. Just like any job, I probably work maybe nine hours a day. I take breaks during those times. We have some time together and just talk or share things. We have three sit-down meals a day. I have a plan of life in terms of a spiritual life. I do fifteen minutes of spiritual reading a day. I do half an hour of prayer in the morning, and then another half an hour in the afternoon. I say the rosary. But these things are all worked out through my day, so it's not like I have a holy hour — a few minutes here and there. And then I usually finish work and have an hour or so for personal things. But compare that with a mother of a family who has no time. It's demanding in a certain sense, but it's not.

Q: What's your social life like?

Marianne: I have friends who I try to keep in contact with. We also have a lot of apostolic activities with girls who work at Shellbourne, the conference center of Opus Dei in Indiana where I live. We have cooking classes and things like that that I participate in. I also go out with friends during my free time.

Q: Does it make you mad or get you irritated that there's sort of this bias against the work of the home?

Marianne: Well I think it's unfortunate, and it used to make me mad when I was younger, but now I just look at society and how things have fallen apart in terms of home life, the family, the breakdown of the family, and I realize how important it is to have your mom there at home.

Sure, your mom can work. I'm not saying anything about mothers who go out and work. But there's got to be priorities. I mean the family's got to come first. The work of the mother, the work of the home really holds the family together. It adds to the character of the family members, because you're raising children to be members of society. I deal with a lot of young people, and I see a lot of very young, sad people. And I can't imagine having the problems that these kids have now. Maybe their parents are divorced, or they're both working, and kids really don't have an outlet to talk. I'm sure their parents do love them, but the pace of the world is very fast, and sometimes the kids fall through the cracks.

Q: What gives you joy in your life?

Marianne: I guess doing my work and doing my work well for love of God. That's the whole mission behind Opus Dei. But also I see that by doing my work for love of God, I'm doing it to serve others. And what really makes me happy is to serve others, because I'm sure if we all really think about it, the happiest times in our lives were times that we weren't thinking about ourselves and we were taking care of others. And so that really is what gives me joy, to be able to serve people and to make them happy. And by doing that, I am also serving God.

FIFTEEN

The Role of Married Women

Supernumeraries

Most of the members of Opus Dei are supernumeraries, that is, men and women who are married or who plan to marry. All the members of Opus Dei share the same vocation. The supernumeraries live the same life of prayer and receive the same spiritual formation as that of the other members, but their main concern is typically their spouse and family. That's the most important area of their life they need to sanctify.

They, too, like the numeraries, numerary assistants, and associates, are called to give to others what they receive, that is, all the Christian formation they receive from Opus Dei. In doing so, they simply do not have the same level of availability the single members have. St. Josemaría describes married supernumeraries this way:

The majority of the members of Opus Dei are married people, so in this field I can speak from the experience of many years of priestly activity in many countries. For the married members of Opus Dei human love and marriage duties are part of their divine vocation. Opus Dei has made of marriage a divine way, a vocation, and this has many consequences for personal holiness and for apostolate. I have spent almost forty years preaching the vocational meaning of marriage. More than once I have had occasion to see faces light up as men and women, who had thought that in their lives a dedication to God was incompatible with a noble and pure human love, heard me say that marriage is a divine path on earth!

The purpose of marriage is to help married people sanctify themselves and others. For this reason they receive a special grace in the sacrament which Jesus Christ instituted. Those who are called to the married state will, with the grace of God, find within their state everything they need to be holy, to identify themselves each day more with Jesus Christ, and to lead those with whom they live to God.

That is why I always look upon Christian homes with hope and affection, upon all the families which are the fruit of the Sacrament of Matrimony. They are a shining witness of the great divine mystery of Christ's loving union with His Church which St. Paul calls *sacramentum magnum,* a great sacrament (Eph. 5:32). We must strive so that these cells of Christianity may be born and may develop with a desire for holiness, conscious of the fact that the Sacrament of Initiation — Baptism — confers on all Christians a divine mission that each must fulfill in his own walk of life.

Christian couples should be aware that they are called to sanctify themselves and to sanctify others, that they are called to be apostles and that their first apostolate is in the home. They should understand that founding a family, educating their children, and exercising a Christian influence in society, are supernatural tasks. The effectiveness and the success of their life — their happiness — depends to a great extent on their awareness of their specific mission.

But they mustn't forget that the secret of married happiness lies in everyday things, not in daydreams. It lies in finding the hidden joy of coming home in the evening, in affectionate relations with their children, in the everyday work in which the whole family co-operates; in good humor in the face of difficulties that should be met with a sporting spirit; in making the best use of all the advantages that civilization offers to help us rear children, to make the house pleasant and life more simple.

I constantly tell those who have been called by God to form a home to love one another always, to love each other with the love of their youth. Anyone who thinks that love ends when the worries and difficulties that life brings with it begin has a poor idea of marriage, which is a sacrament and an ideal and a vocation. It is precisely then that love grows strong. Torrents of worries and difficulties are incapable of drowning true love because people who sacrifice themselves generously together are brought closer by their sacrifice. As Scripture says . . . a host of difficulties, physical and moral . . . "cannot extinguish love" (Cant. 8:7).*

---

*St. Josemaría Escrivá, *Conversations* (New York: Scepter Publishers, 2008), no. 91.

SIXTEEN

Living the Beatitudes

Interview with a Peruvian Immigrant
and Childcare Provider

Doris Cerna moved to the United States from Peru with her husband and two small boys in December of 1990. She has been a supernumerary member of Opus Dei since 1985. She met Opus Dei through her dance. In Peru, she had been a member of a professional dance group for ten years. Their specialty was Peruvian folk dancing. She had a friend who loved Peruvian folk dancing who asked if she would come and perform at a center of Opus Dei in Peru. Doris did, and that was the first time she set foot in a center of Opus Dei.

Sometime after that she was invited to attend a retreat. She did, and she loved it. Doris recalls:

After the retreat I was very moved. I wanted to read more about the founder so I got the book *The Founder of Opus Dei.* By the end I thought, "This is what I want." So I asked if I could join. But they made me wait, so first I got married, and then after that I joined Opus Dei.

She married in August 1985 and joined Opus Dei in December of that year; she was twenty-nine years old at the time. She and her husband have lived in California since moving to the United States. With her two sons in college now, she and her husband are hardly empty-nesters. Doris runs a childcare center in her home. At the time of this interview, she had about six little children on the premises. And the house could not be more peaceful and serene. It seems an impossible feat.

Q: So what has been your experience in Opus Dei?

Doris: My first five years in Opus Dei I was living in Peru. When we moved here I was totally alone with my family — just my husband and my two kids, but not my extended family, so I found the Work really helpful.

I was totally involved, and I had peace, a lot of comfort. All this formation when I was just new in the Work helped me to survive here [San Jose, California] because I was alone with nobody to help me to cope. And I learned how to cook here and I learned how to be a mom because I was alone with my boys. It was very hard, but I got support from the priests of the Work* and the numerary from whom I received spiritual advice. And reading, doing a lot of reading. So the Work was my second home.

Q: Tell me about your business. Tell me how you run a business here.

Doris: When I moved to this country I decided to study English. I went to college. I arrived here December 9, and by the

---

*Priestly Society of the Holy Cross: "The Priestly Society of the Holy Cross is an association of clergy intrinsically united to Opus Dei, which currently has about four thousand members. It is made up of the clergy of the Prelature, who are automatically members, and other diocesan priests and (transitional) deacons. The Prelate of Opus Dei is its president" (see *www.opusdei.org*, Priestly Society of the Holy Cross section).

first week of January I was already enrolled in Foothill College, which is very close to my home. At the same time my boys were attending preschool there and I started to help in the preschool, to volunteer, and I liked it. That was something new for me. I never thought that I wanted to be a teacher. So when I was taking my English class and they asked me if I wanted to choose a career, I decided to be a teacher. I was taking classes, but just one class per quarter, because my boys came first.

I managed to go to college, to work part-time in the children's center, and at the same time help my boys. When the boys moved to elementary school, I kept that job. I was in that job for nine years working as an assistant teacher.

I was learning a lot. And then I thought, I'm going to do this in a family setting so that I can still do my job as a mom and take care of the boys. And at the same time I can help my husband and have a business. I've had my business now for four years.

Q: How many children do you have in your childcare?

Doris: I'm licensed to have twelve, and right now it's almost full. I just have a couple of kids who are coming for a few hours because they are little. But most of the time the school is full and I have a waiting list, and people are calling all the time.

I try to refer them to friends I know who have spaces in their day-care centers. We have a network. We want these families to go to nice places because there are a lot of family day-care centers, but some are not really safe. We want the parents to go to really good places where the kids can be very safe.

Q: How do you think your vocation to Opus Dei impacts your business and your work?

Doris: This is the place I need to sanctify first. And in doing my job the best I can, I can sanctify myself because I'm offering this to the Lord.

Q: Are the people who send their children here in Opus Dei?

Doris: No.

Q: Are they all Catholic?

Doris: No, I have just a few Catholics; most of them are Christians. I have one lady who does not practice any religion. She's from Syria, but she is not Christian or Muslim, and her husband is Jewish. They are a very nice couple, and they are involved; they want to help.

And then I have one couple from India. They are not Catholic, but her child has been here for almost two years, and he wants to know more about Jesus and is happy about Christmas. The parents are very open.

Q: In terms of the day-to-day work and the way you deal with the children, how does your vocation to Opus Dei have an impact?

Doris: First of all, this is my opportunity to practice the Beatitudes, like patience, because to have seven or eight toddlers together at the same time is very crazy, so that gives me and my colleagues the opportunity to have lots of patience. It's a challenge because sometimes we can lose our temper, and we need to control it; we need to give a good example.

This job also gives me the opportunity to teach the kids the Beatitudes like meekness and to be kind with each other, to be attentive about other kids' needs and to help each other to work as a group.

I have to make sure the kids send that message home. Each month I send a letter, and I tell the parents what I need for that month, what activities we're going to do. I tell them a little bit about the Beatitudes, and I ask the parents to try to talk to me so they can follow what we are doing here. I want them to follow at home because the kids need to have the same language here and at home. Otherwise, they get confused.

Q: And are the parents open to that?

Doris: They are open. Most of these couples have only one or two kids, and they're always complaining. So I decided to have a meeting with each of them. Every four or five months I sit down, especially with the moms, and talk about how they are doing at home, how business is, and this and that. In that time, I can tell them how important it is for them to be focused on their kids.

I tell them that I am glad to care for the children, and I suggest that when they are home, they should try, as much as possible, to be involved with their child. Because later on these kids are going to be five, six, seven, and that's it. Otherwise, they are not going to have good bonds between the moms and the kids because most of the time the kids are with us.

Sometimes they call us Mom, and I say, "No, I'm not your mom, I'm your teacher. And Mommy's going to be here very soon." They need to know.

Q: *Do you think it's wrong that mothers work when their children are little?*

Doris: It all depends on the circumstances, because if they really need to help their husbands, I suggest that, as much as possible, they work part-time so they can earn some money, but can spend the rest of the time with their kids. Most of the kids who are kindergarten age go to school only three hours a day. That's by law. So I suggest that they work in the morning and then go to school, pick up the kids, and then go home, cook, have lunch together, get ready for the afternoon with their husbands coming, and nobody's going to be stressed.

Some mothers work in the morning, and then they take some work home, so they can put in the rest of their hours at home at night when the kids are sleeping. My experience is that it's better to invest now, giving as much as possible to your kids: love, time, and everything. And then you are okay; you are not going to have problems when they are teenagers or when they are adults. Most of the problems right now are because the kids are really lonely, very sad. They don't get affection from their parents; they are insecure. And when they go to school they have to live with a lot of pressure: peer pressure, lots of homework, sports, and this and that. It's too much for the kids; it's too much.

They need to be kids. They need to be able to play with Mom, with Dad. Sometimes moms and dads don't have time to play after they get home from their jobs. I think that according to the circumstances, it's okay if they have to go to work full-time, but one of them can look for a part-time job. That's my advice.

But if that's not possible, they need to figure out how to work together, husband and wife, so when one of them is working, the other one can be with the kids.

Q: *Do the parents know that you're in Opus Dei?*

Doris: They know because when the book *The Da Vinci Code* came out, a journalist from ABC News came to the house and we talked about Opus Dei. I asked permission of the parents for the kids to be on TV. And everybody said, Sure, they wanted their kids to be on the TV. We were on ABC in San Francisco.

I explained to each family: "Look, this is something personal, but I need to share with you because right now, it's everywhere. And I just want to know if your kids can be in the news." I explained that this was my opportunity to explain what Opus Dei is.

And they were very happy with this, that their kids were going to be on TV, and to find out that I was member of Opus Dei, and they had no problem with that. I gave them the website information so they could do research to see what Opus Dei is.

Q: *Is your husband in Opus Dei also?*

Doris: No, he's not a member, but he loves Opus Dei a lot. My boys received a good Catholic education. They both know about vocation because we talked about it. They know that I never push them, because that's something that they need to deal with on their own.

Q: *How do you fit your plan of life? You have a busy day, right? What time does your day-care center open?*

Doris: 8:00 a.m. I attend 6:30 a.m. Mass, then after Mass, I spend prayer time with our Lord. And then I come back and have my breakfast, and we open the school.

Then around 10:30 a.m. the kids go for a walk; two teachers help with these children. They go to the park or someplace, and at that time I pray some more. Then in the afternoon, after my lunch, I go for a walk. I need to go for my daily walk and pray my rosary.

I have a 6:00 p.m. dinner with my husband and then I can do my spiritual reading.

Q: *How do you evangelize, which is part of your vocation?*

Doris: I try to have a really strong friendship with the mothers. I talk a lot with each one, so when they come in the morning or leave in the afternoon, I try to show interest in what they're doing with business or their career, and I try to get to know a little bit about their lives. So this is my personal apostolate.

Q: *Do you pray for them?*

Doris: Pray? Yes. I pray when I'm changing diapers or I'm tired or my back hurts because all day I am changing diapers. Sometimes I'm just so tired that I say, This is for the future vocations, and I keep going. It's 5:00 p.m., and these kids are still running around. And I'm just totally exhausted.

Q: *How many people do you have working for you?*

Doris: I have [Dulia], who's from Peru, and [Millicent], who's a teacher from Singapore. And my husband comes to help us out. So four — we are four.

Q: *And how long do the children usually stay with you?*

Doris: From 8:00 a.m. to 5:00 p.m. Usually they come when they are six months old; they leave when they are ready to go to kindergarten.

Q: *You don't usually have people who pull their kids out?*

Doris: No.

Q: *Do you make a good living doing it?*

Doris: Yes, it helps. It's not a whole lot of money because I have to pay the other two teachers. But I think it's better than going outside as a teacher to find a job.

Q: *Is there anything else you want to tell me?*

Doris: Yes. Women in Opus Dei are very strong. You have to try to do your really, really best because it's for the Lord your God. I think women in Opus Dei are very happy people.

Q: *Why is that?*

Doris: Because we receive so much and we can use that to help others.

SEVENTEEN

All Professions Are Open

In the early 1930s, St. Josemaría began to speak out clearly on the equality of men and women, saying that all work, all noble professional fields, should be open to women. He also took the argument one step further, proclaiming that the work of the home is a professional work that deserves to be respected and practiced as such. Even today, this latter notion remains lost on many who consider themselves champions of the women's movement. While St. Josemaría may not have been in a position to propose public policy to support these views, he certainly did propose ethical, philosophical, and theological arguments promoting the dignity of all work, and especially the work of the home and raising a family:

> In terms of fundamentals, one can in fact speak of equal rights which should be legally recognized, both in civil and ecclesiastical law. Women, like men, possess the dignity of being persons and children of God. Nevertheless, on this basis of fundamental equality, each must achieve what is proper to him or her. In this sense a woman's emancipation means that she should have a real possibility of developing her own potentialities to the fullest extent — those which she has personally and

those which she has in common with other women. Equal rights and equal opportunities before the law do not suppress this diversity, which enriches all mankind. They presuppose and encourage it. . . .

To fulfill [her] mission, a woman has to develop her own personality and not let herself be carried away by a naive desire to imitate, which, as a rule, would tend to put her in an inferior position and leave her unique qualities unfulfilled. If she is a mature person, with a character and mind of her own, she will indeed accomplish the mission to which she feels called, whatever it may be. Her life and work will be really constructive, fruitful and full of meaning, whether she spends the day dedicated to her husband and children or whether, having given up the idea of marriage for a noble reason, she has given herself fully to other tasks.*

Housework is something of primary importance. Besides, all work can have the same supernatural quality. There are no great or mean tasks. All are great if they are done with love. Those which are considered great become small when the Christian meaning of life is lost sight of. On the other hand, there are apparently small things that can in fact be very great because of their real effects.

As far as I am concerned, the work of one of my daughters in Opus Dei who works in domestic employment is just as important as that of one who has a title. In either case all I am concerned about is that the work they do should be a means and an occasion for personal

---

*St. Josemaría Escrivá, *Conversations* (New York: Scepter Publishers, 2008), no. 87.

sanctification and the sanctification of their neighbor. The importance depends on whether a woman in her own job and position in life is becoming more holy, and fulfilling with greater love the mission she has received from God.

Before God all men have the same standing, whether they are university professors, shop-assistants, secretaries, laborers, or farmers. All souls are equal. Only, at times, the souls of simple and unaffected people are more beautiful; and certainly those who are more intimate with God the Father, God the Son, and God the Holy Spirit are always more pleasing to our Lord.*

---

*St. Josemaría Escrivá, *Conversations* (New York: Scepter Publishers, 2008), no. 109.

EIGHTEEN

Changing Diapers for God

MIT Graduate Who Raises Her
Eight Children Full-Time

Margaret Kalb has been a supernumerary since 1997. She is the mother of eight children. She met Opus Dei as an undergraduate at the Massachusetts Institute of Technology (MIT). She graduated with a bachelor's degree in music. She also met her husband, Art, at MIT. He's an electrical engineer. A bit on the countercultural side, they married at the end of Margaret's junior year. Here's her story:

I was one of the first in my family to have a chance to go to college. My parents never had a chance to go. My father never even graduated from high school. And then I got into MIT! Everyone was so excited! My mother had visions of a glamorous career for me, but then one day I came home and said I was getting married and planning to raise a family.

When Art and I met, I was a freshman, and he was a junior. We were friends almost from day one at school, but I was dating somebody else. We started dating in December of his senior year. Right before Christmas vacation, he suddenly had a strong motivation to stick around MIT for another year or two; otherwise he would be leaving school that May or June. And he said, "Well, maybe I should apply for grad school really quickly." So he applied for the master's program at MIT.

Art was accepted into the master's program, and this allowed the two to keep dating.

We really liked each other. We were already very close friends and very much on the same wavelength regarding the nature of marriage. And we got engaged about three months later. Prior to getting engaged, I was on the career path, or so I thought. I was actually working on two bachelor's degrees because as a general rule it's quite difficult to work in music full-time and support yourself. You usually need something else to pay the bills and the rent. So I was really over my head, working on this second degree at the same time in information technology. That was the game plan. And then I started going out with Art.

Before we were engaged or anything, we were talking about the whole question of large families. Neither of us was in the Work, but we both attended activities for young college kids. We'd both received some pretty solid formation on the Catholic understanding of marriage and also met some very impressive people who were raising large families themselves.

So we were sitting around talking about this and were wondering about combining a big family with the wife's career. I just started thinking out loud and I said, "Well, I guess I don't see the point in having a big family if you're just going to pay somebody else to take care of them." Then I threw my hand over my mouth in horror, saying, "What did I just say?!" There went the career right out the window!

I was just thinking out loud. But it was true. As a practical matter, the kind of salary I could make would never pay for day care for a lot of kids. In the United States, unless you're a brain surgeon or something, child care for a large number of children is not an option financially.

So with that she dropped her second major and focused on music. She explains how Opus Dei figured into her relationship with Art and her decision process.

I showed up at MIT having been raised a Catholic and having attended Catholic school my entire life. We went to Mass every Sunday without fail, even while traveling. But my parents were somewhat private people, and we were not given to very loud or exuberant expressions of faith.

Unfortunately my religious education was pretty awful. I think my mother and father really didn't realize how much Catholic education had changed soon after Vatican II. They really didn't realize how much content had been sucked out of Catholic education at that point. It mostly consisted of, "God loves me and let's make felt banners." Very little meat.

Meanwhile, I'd been really pushing myself academically through high school. I had skipped my sophomore year, I was studying Shakespeare and physics. I was valedictorian of my class and heading off for MIT. By contrast the Catholic faith seemed childish and silly because I had never heard any sort of an intellectually meaningful defense of the faith, ever, from anybody. I got to college already wondering what I was going to do about all this "stuff."

I still went to Mass on Sunday because it was so ingrained in me from home — if you're Catholic, you must go to Mass on Sunday. And then I accidentally got roped into it really quickly because the girl who had been directing the music at the 5:00 p.m. Mass just sort of fell off the face of the earth about two weeks into the semester. So all of a sudden I was directing the music and playing piano at the 5:00 p.m. Mass. I had this obligation to be there independently of whether I was in the mood for it or not. I needed to be there because other people were depending on me. I started to feel hypocritical. I was going through all these motions and doing all this stuff, and I didn't know if I believed any of it. By the end of my first semester I decided I was either going to figure this out, this Catholic business, or else just drop it.

In parallel with that I had joined the pro-life group right away when I got to MIT. That was the one thing that had stuck with me even though I had really started to reject a lot of what the Church taught. My mother was and is extremely pro-life. There were thought-provoking articles and magazines around the house, and we talked about it. When I joined the pro-life group, one of the first people I met was Ann, this numerary who lived at Bayridge [a student residence of Opus Dei in Boston]. She was brilliant, and she really impressed me. I wanted to hang around with her because she was so smart.

At the time, of course, I didn't realize what a horrible, arrogant little punk I was. Once I was talking to Ann and shooting my mouth off about how the Church teaches us all these stupid things and needs to get into the twentieth century. I even said, "The only thing the Pope and I agree about is pro-life, that's it." Ann asked me, "Well, have you ever read anything that the Pope has written?" And I said, "No, but I don't have to. I read the newspapers, and they tell me what he says, so I know what he says."

God bless her, Ann never lost patience with me. She realized that despite my mouthing off, I was trying to sort all this stuff out. She invited me to go on a retreat, and I went. So that was how I met the Work, and that retreat turned out to be a pivotal event for me. It was so odd: I wasn't expecting it to turn my whole life upside-down.

I went on this retreat and even before the first meditation had started, Ann showed me where the chapel was. I walked into the oratory, and I knelt down to say a prayer. My parents had always said whenever you come into a Church you should always kneel down and say a prayer.

So, okay, I knelt down, I said a prayer. And I said to myself, I'd better say something, so I started saying the Our Father. Actually, this was different from my normal routine, because the chapel at MIT where I was going for Mass every Saturday was not a Catholic chapel. It was just a nondenominational space, so the Blessed Sacrament was not there.

I certainly didn't understand the full depth of it, but I knew there was a difference between the chapel at MIT and the oratory at the retreat house. At 4:30 p.m. on Saturday at MIT the priest would show up, pull out the tablecloth, hang up a crucifix, and we were good to go. There was no sanctuary light or anything like that. So, yes, I knew that something was different.

I knelt down and I started saying the Our Father, and I was just barely into it when I got hit by what a friend of mine calls "the Holy Two-by-Four." I just got this whack on the head from God. When I got to, "Thy will be done," it suddenly hit me, and I stopped. God's will? When had I ever considered God's will? All the enormous decisions I'd been making over the last year or so — where to go to college, what dorm to live in, what classes to take — these were essentially the first decisions I'd made in my life as an adult, independently of my parents. And God was supposed to have a say in it?

This was the "Holy two-by-four." All of a sudden it dawned on me: God had plans. He had plans for everybody. He had a plan for me, and I didn't know what it was. And I had been making all these huge decisions without ever taking that into consideration. It was an enormous shock. But after that I was raring to go. A minute or two later, Father Sal [Ferigle] came in and gave the first meditation. I was just drinking in all this formation the whole weekend. It was a complete eye-opener for me.

I pretty much spent every free minute on the retreat reading whatever I could get my hands on. I had already had a complete change of heart on things even though I didn't necessarily understand the reasoning behind some of them. The one that really sticks with me was contraception. I remember talking to Ann about it at the end of the retreat. I had already made this leap of faith — the Church taught that it was wrong, and I couldn't argue with that, but I didn't really feel able to explain it to anybody else yet. I realized I had like a ton of work to do, catching up on everything I hadn't been taught in twelve years of Catholic education.

After the retreat I was very regular over at Bayridge for anything I could attend. It took me actually a while to figure out that there was a schedule to the activities at Bayridge. I knew that some Thursdays I would show up and there was something longer, and those were the evenings of recollection. And then the other Thursdays I would show up and there was something shorter and the priest would just give a meditation and he'd be available for confessions.

I was trying to make up for lost time, for all the formation I'd missed. Fortunately, that summer I stayed in Boston to work on campus. I worked during the days, but I had my evenings and weekends free. That summer Father Sal gave a really well-done presentation of the basics of the Catholic faith — the Creed, the Ten Commandments, the sacraments — and I was there every week with my notebook in hand. It filled in a lot of the gaps and taught me a lot of fairly basic things I'd never even heard of before.

This course is required before or during your process of joining Opus Dei to make sure you have a solid doctrinal background. From my point of view, that is actually very much a part of the Work's devotion to freedom, the fact that the vocation is a very free choice. You need to be very informed to make a very free choice. Only after you have all this information at your disposal can you freely decide to say yes or no to it. You're not just saying yes blindly.

Margaret did not join Opus Dei until well after she graduated from college and already had several children.

It took quite a while. I was married and had three children before I joined Opus Dei. In the back of my mind I think I always knew that someday I was going to join the Work, just not now (that is, in college). So much of the vocation appealed to me. I thought it would be great. These were such cool people, and you got to take all these classes, and it was very appealing.

Her husband joined the Work while still at MIT.

In fact, he joined just a short time before we got engaged. It actually made me very resentful of the Work for a while because all of his time was suddenly getting sucked up with taking all these formational classes. Of course, you don't have a lot of free time to start with at MIT. Life revolves around problem sets and papers and lab experiments. Then on top of it, he was taking these extra classes. Meanwhile, I was trying to plan a wedding. I didn't drive, I didn't have a car, so I needed his help to go look at reception halls. It was annoying for a while.

Did Opus Dei encourage her to have a large family?

Opus Dei encourages us to live as Catholics in the fullest sense of the word. And Catholics at the barest minimum should not be using artificial contraceptives and are encouraged to be as generous in having children as their circumstances allow. In practice that means a variety of things. I know plenty of married gals in the Work who have had only one or two children. Perhaps they struggled for years and years to even have one baby, and that was all they were able to have. There are others who found out that medically the pregnancies were so hard on them that they couldn't, shouldn't have another baby because doing so would have threatened their health or threatened their life.

So it's not all about cranking out a baby every two years at all. It's really a question of circumstances, which I wish more people understood. It's a little embarrassing for me, in a way, because I'm afraid people are going to look at me and say, "Oh, these Catholics. See, that's what happens if you really live seriously as a Catholic. You have to have another baby every two years." In reality, Art and I decided every time that we wanted to have another baby.

Once you've gotten the formation and you know right from wrong and you know what the Church teaches, you're still morally your own person, and you have to make those decisions for yourself. It is really impressive. One of the things I like about the Work is that respect for freedom is not just lip service. They really mean it. They really, really do.

Margaret thought about possibly joining as a numerary before she joined as a supernumerary.

I thought about it for a while when I was wrestling with the whole marriage question. After the Holy Two-by-Four retreat, I made this other retreat a year later, praying and agonizing over whether I was supposed to marry Art or not, or whether I should really become a numerary. I did think about the numerary vocation very briefly, but I realized that I was definitely supposed to get married. I don't think I could live in a center, for instance. I'm not a schedule person at all.

And believe me, there's a schedule here too, but it's different. I certainly have to get up on time. I have to get my kids up too. I don't know if I have the kind of personality needed to live in a center, but that's the discernment that people have to make when they're looking at their vocation. People need to ask: Are you a match for a numerary vocation or not?

On the whole question of feeling free or not free, I don't know how to address it except that I've never personally felt not free in any regard, any regard at all. All I can say is if people really felt that they weren't free, my best guess is that it was just a mismatch from the start. Maybe they weren't ready to live the kind of a lifestyle that comes with living in the center.

What led Margaret to finally join Opus Dei?

It was all Father Sal's doing. He died. That was what finally
did it. We lived out here in California and couldn't go to the
funeral in Boston. He had officiated at our wedding. Art and
I both loved him dearly. I was pretty broken up about it. So
anyway, his funeral was on a Saturday. He died on Thursday,
January 9, and his funeral was on January 11. That was the
day I joined the Work.

We found out the funeral was in Boston at 11:00 a.m.,
which in California time would be 8:00 a.m. So we dressed
up all the children and we went to 8:00 a.m. Mass at Our
Lady of Peace up the road to pray for Father Sal. We couldn't
really be at his funeral, but we could still, in a way, go to his
funeral from California. And sometime during the Mass I
realized: I can't dodge this anymore. I have to go join the
Work. Today. Now.

I was in a cooperator's circle, and I was going to recollections, but it was kind of hit or miss, because I had all these
babies at home. I'd had three babies in two-and-a-half years.
I was knee-deep in diapers. I didn't realize at the time how
swamped I was. My oldest child had special needs, although
he wasn't diagnosed at the time. He wasn't speaking, the
fifteen-month-old wasn't speaking either, and obviously the
baby wasn't speaking. The oldest one wasn't potty trained
yet either, because of his condition. So everybody was in
diapers, and nobody was talking.

But when Father Sal died and we "went to his funeral,"
I realized, "Oh my gosh, I have to join the Work right
now." We had already planned to take the kids to breakfast. There's an IHOP right next door to the church, so we
took the kids, and I told Art at breakfast that we needed

to head up to Charwick [a women's center of Opus Dei in California] afterward. He was kind of surprised.

The director of the local center at the time was a little startled too, because I called just to make sure somebody would be home and then we drove up there. She and I had talked about it in theory before, if I ever did join the Work, but I had never decided I really wanted to. Then I showed up on the doorstep, wanting to join right away.

I was told I needed to write a letter to the vicar, requesting admission to Opus Dei. I started writing this and explaining about how Father Sal had just died, and I wanted to join the Work because of Father Sal. And Peggy [the director] double checked with me: "You want to do this, right? You're not just doing this because of Father Sal?" It was the whole question of freedom again. She wanted to make sure.

It wasn't my feeling guilty that he had died and I'd never joined when he was alive or something crazy like that. It was none of that. Really, I think Father Sal was cashing in his favors once he'd gotten to heaven and was enjoying himself walking around whacking people on the heads with the Holy Two-by-Four.

Managing to live her plan of life every day with so many little children can be challenging.

It's so hard. And you have to understand, every time I have a baby, it blows my whole plan of life again. I have to start all over again with each baby. One of the really helpful things, though, about the spirit of the Work is "Begin again." So it's okay that I'm basically starting from scratch again. I'll have been in the Work for ten years in January, and still just in the last week or two, I'm starting to get my prayer back into my schedule. And the baby is seven weeks old! So the first six weeks there was no way I could do it.

The people in the Work encourage me to do as much as I feel I can do, and then that's good enough. "Okay, well just ask God to take care of the rest because he knows." I want to be praying more. And I'm trying to get it back in again now.

We asked her how she thinks her vocation impacts her being a stay-at-home mom.

I think it really helps in a lot of ways. For one thing, being a homemaker is associated with a lot of drudgery, and rightly so. It is pure drudgery. Laundry — you wash the same things over and over and over again. You fold them and put them away and the kids get them dirty and they go back in the laundry again.

And I wash the same dishes every night, and they get dirty again and I have to wash them again, and they get put away again. And I spend two hours cooking a meal, and twenty minutes after it's been put on the table, it's all gone. It really is a lot of work. And if it didn't have a deeper meaning to it I'd probably be insane by now. The fact that it does, thank God, have this deeper spiritual meaning to it, makes all the difference. I'm washing dishes for God. I'm changing diapers for God.

It helps me realize that I'm participating in the Communion of Saints. Sometimes I feel kind of frustrated because there are all these things in the world that I would love to go out and fix, like abortion. I was so into the pro-life movement in college. At that time, I actually could go out and pray at the clinics and picket and do all these crazy things, and write letters to the editor and so on. Right now I can't do any of that.

My vocation teaches me that I can't be out there on the front lines, but I can still wash the dishes for an end to abortion. I can do that. Or trying to help those people in Darfur who are going through such awful, awful things. I can't do anything tangible about that either, but I can fold laundry for them.

It's called the Communion of Saints. The way I sometimes explain it is that by offering up our work, we can sort of make "spiritual deposits" in a "spiritual bank" and then when our brothers and sisters need that, they can draw on it. When someone needs those graces, they're available. And I can offer my work up for them, which probably sounds like crazy talk for somebody who's not a Christian.

I've heard some interesting stories about it. We have a custom in the Work of saying at least a Memorare each day, for whoever needs it the most. I love that custom because it is such a concrete way of living the Communion of Saints. I don't know who it is, but somebody, somewhere needs help, so I'm going to say this Memorare.

I heard this cool story once of one fellow who was in Opus Dei. I think he had to eject from his plane in the Falkland Islands War. He was in the water and really not at all sure that he was going to survive, except that he knew that people were saying all these Memorares and that they were saying them for him, even if they didn't know it. All these people all over the world were praying for him. Very cool.

Margaret has tried to keep a list of people she wants to pray for every day.

I did and I think it got wiped off my Palm Pilot at some point. But I kind of know. I just shuffle through it. I'm probably not as organized about it as some people are. I'm sure there are people who are much better about this than I am. But I'll get phone calls and, oh, yes, so-and-so, her brother just died, and then one of my husband's cousins just died this last week — different things. You pray for them, and then somebody else is getting treated for cancer, and then somebody else is just going through a hard time right now. And then I have my own houseful of kids to pray for.

She explains what she believes praying for her friends actually does for them.

I probably won't find out until I get to heaven, and I hope to get there. A couple of years ago I was at a party and finally met a guy that I had seen at Mass for years and years. So I knew he had to be a pretty solid Catholic if he was going to daily Mass all the time even though I'd never met him before.

So we were at somebody's first communion party and were talking and got on to this whole thing of the crisis of formation, how people aren't being taught the faith in Catholic schools anymore. And so I told him an encapsulated version of my story and how a friend got me to go on a retreat, and I had a sudden conversion experience, just out of the blue. And he said to me, he said, "She must have been praying for you a lot before that retreat, a lot." I had never thought about it before; it was very profound. And I responded, "Yes, you're probably right. She probably was." I didn't know she was praying for me before that. I had no idea. I didn't know that. But when I was — when the time was right, when God knew I was ready for it, that's when I got hit with it, so, I have to assume.

Margaret comments how apostolate works for her and in Opus Dei in general.

Apostolate is first of all done in friendship.

My goal is to get people closer to God. And hopefully for some of them that will mean Opus Dei if that's what God has in mind for them, if that's how God wants them to get close to him. But that certainly won't be the case for everybody. For some of them it's just a question of getting them closer to God. It might just mean helping them to realize that they need to start going to Mass again every Sunday if they've stopped going. Or maybe they might want to go to confession a couple times a year. You start with where people are and try to help them get going.

Margaret explains her circle and what she gets out of it.

The circle meets every week. And it's very structured. There is a reading from the day's Gospel. And the person giving the circle will make a brief comment on it and draw something out of it that we can apply to our daily lives, which is really helpful because we're supposed to be encountering Christ in our daily lives and reading the New Testament every day.

Hearing somebody else's interesting little insight into that particular passage from the Gospel is already helpful right there. Then we'll have two talks on topics that vary widely. They'll usually cover some practice of piety, like the things of the plan of life. So they could be talking about prayer or the Mass, or the Memorare, which is very helpful because you have to keep these things fresh. You can get into a rut if you're not careful.

Margaret explains the preparation and authority the people who give the circles have.

Circles of supernumeraries are usually given by a numerary or an associate, although some supernumeraries also periodically give the circle to other supernumeraries in their group. Supernumeraries usually give circles to cooperators of Opus Dei. And there's a grace of state* that comes from having a vocation. They also have had formation. A lot of it is very practical. This is somebody else who's been struggling through the plan of life for years, and this is what she's gleaned out of it. I think there's a real grace that operates when somebody is told to give a circle or give a talk about something.

I will get asked to give talks at recollections and things like that about some topic or another. Between doing a little bit of research and taking the topic to my prayer, I have to figure that God is going to use me as his instrument to say what these people need to hear. And it works, and the circles work.

Opus Dei in her life influences how she approaches raising her children.

The Christian formation offered by Opus Dei reminds us of good Catholic principles for raising children. Then each

---

*Graces of State: These are graces that "accompany the exercise of the responsibilities of the Christian life and of the ministries within the Church" (see *Catechism of the Catholic Church,* no. 2004).

family decides how to apply those principles; no one can tell someone else how to raise their kids.

These basic principles like cheerfulness, order, justice apply at home, and I need to be teaching those to my kids. And I'm happy that sometimes I get reminded of that because it's much easier on rough days to just give in: "Here, kid, have a cookie. Just shut up and leave me alone and have your cookie and go, whatever." It helps me a lot to be reminded of the need to teach my kids to live virtue and for me to be reminded to live the virtues I need to teach them.

One of the definitions of being a saint is exercising the virtues to a heroic degree. Well, there's plenty of room for heroism in saying no to the tantrumming four-year-old when it would be so much easier to just say yes and just get some peace for ten minutes. And to say no again, knowing that you're going to be listening to more screaming and more kicking. There's a heroism in that. The encouragement I get to do that from the Work is supremely helpful in that regard.

As the kids get older and we're starting to navigate all these bigger issues like "Can I go out with my friends?" "How often can I go out with my friends?" "Can I wear makeup to school?" "Is this skirt too short?" "Can I wear this?" Nobody's giving me specifics like "Your children can only go out with their friends once a week from 2:00 p.m. to 5:00 p.m."

The encouragement and support I receive from Opus Dei help me have the mind-set of trying to evaluate these decisions from the point of view of what is good for the children in the long term. Is this going to help them be saints someday? Is this decision going to be good for our family as a whole. That's helpful.

Opus Dei has a positive impact on her marriage.

It is also helpful to be reminded to try to live virtues to a heroic degree. There's real room for selfishness, I think, in a marriage. It's easy after the first couple of years to slide back into selfishness and laziness. Again, I'm getting encouragement and spiritual direction plus additional formation from spiritual reading and spending time in prayer. These mitigate the tendency toward laziness and selfishness; they really do. What can really be the death knell for marriage is when people just slide into these parallel tracks. They might be living alongside each other but are not really trying to achieve a level of self-sacrificing love, really going the extra mile. I think it's also very helpful that my husband is in the Work.

One of the things I love about the Work is that we have access to really good classes and talks and teachers to learn what the Catholic faith teaches. I think it is so cool especially in this day and age because my generation was so poorly catechized. And once you've had enough of this formation, you start to see that the whole thing fits together, all the pieces. Christian morality makes such sense.

For a long time I was just pro-life, and I didn't really know or care about anything else. But once you start learning about what the Church teaches about abortion, what the Church teaches about marriage, about economic justice, about — you just pick all these little constellation points, and once you've filled in enough of those gaps all of a sudden you say, "Oh, my gosh, this whole thing makes so much sense." The whole Christian outlook on right and wrong and how the world works really fits together. And there's intellectual grounding to it. It's not just this fluffy thing of being nice or being good, but there's no meat to it. Every year we take a week off to take theology and philosophy classes, which, as a housewife anyway, is such a treat for me.

Getting away is fun; that's part of it. But it's different than getting away to a spa for a week, which I've never done anyway. The other part of it is the intellectual engagement. It's really wonderful, from my point of view, because right now I don't get a whole lot of that at home. I'm changing diapers and things like that. I try. I read. I have interesting conversations with people. But having a focused week like that of just classes is really cool. I like it.

It's so much fun spending time with other supernumeraries at the workshop. You meet such a diverse range of people in the Work it is not even funny. There's a stereotype, I think, of everybody in the Work, that they're all little rosary-praying automatons, and the women are all perfectly coiffed Stepford Wives who never have their hair out of place. That's so not true.

The real people have such interesting backgrounds. I encounter a lot more conformity among supposedly diverse groups of people who all hold the same viewpoint. In the Work we're all Catholic, we all believe what the Church teaches, but then if you start to talk about politics or popular culture, you'll hear stuff across the board. It's fascinating; it's really fascinating.

NINETEEN

Prayer, the Sacraments, and the Christian Spirit of Sacrifice and Poverty

Let us work. Let us work a lot and work well, without forgetting that prayer is our best weapon. That is why I will never tire of repeating that we have to be contemplative souls in the midst of the world, who try to convert their work into prayer. ⃰

While Opus Dei has a lot to do with finding God in one's ordinary work, the bottom line is that even work is understood to be a means to pray, not an end in itself. A vocation to Opus Dei all comes down to prayer, that is, trying to maintain an intimate, ongoing friendship with God. God just wants to be loved. Like all Catholics, people in Opus Dei have enormous resources to support them in their quest to maintain an ongoing, loving relationship with God each day. The sacraments rank on top of those resources. And the most important sacrament is the Eucharist. This is the height of Christian prayer. In the *Compendium of the Catechism of the Catholic Church* we read the following points

---

⃰St. Josemaría Escrivá, *Furrow* (New York: Scepter Publishers, 1992), no. 497.

on the importance of the Eucharist in the life of the Church and the life of all the faithful:

> It is the source and summit of all Christian life. In the Eucharist, the sanctifying action of God in our regard and our worship of him reach their high point. It contains the whole spiritual good of the Church, Christ himself, our Pasch. Communion with divine life and the unity of the People of God are both expressed and effected by the Eucharist. Through the eucharistic celebration we are united already with the liturgy of heaven and we have a foretaste of eternal life.*

> The Eucharist is the very sacrifice of the Body and Blood of the Lord Jesus which he instituted to perpetuate the sacrifice of the cross throughout the ages until his return in glory. Thus he entrusted to his Church this memorial of his death and Resurrection. It is a sign of unity, a bond of charity, a paschal banquet, in which Christ is consumed, the mind is filled with grace, and a pledge of future glory is given to us.**

Members of Opus Dei strive to participate reverently in the celebration of the Eucharist daily. For them, this is the center and root of their life of prayer. It is the quintessential channel of God's grace. It is praying through, with, and in Jesus Christ, as he sacrifices himself once again for our salvation. All prayer and all sacrifice, Catholics believe, have their merit before God because of the action of Jesus Christ in the Eucharist.

---

*Compendium of the Catechism of the Catholic Church, no. 274.
**Compendium of the Catechism of the Catholic Church, no. 271.

Members of Opus Dei also frequently receive the Sacrament of Reconciliation (also known as Confession), typically once a week. Many people who believe that this great Sacrament of God's mercy is necessary for the forgiveness of mortal sin do not realize that it also extremely helpful when one has less grievous sins to confess. This great source of God's grace and mercy strengthens each soul to begin again in her struggle to be holy. The Church encourages all the faithful to go to confession regularly.

Like all Catholics and many Christians and people of other Judeo-Christian creeds, members of Opus Dei also practice a spirit of penance and sacrifice, which is characteristic of Catholicism. It is based on the example and teachings of Jesus Christ, the early Christians, and the tradition of the saints. Another term used for this is "mortification," that is, dying to oneself so that we can live the life of Christ. St. Josemaría characterized the kind of spirit of penance someone can struggle to live in daily life this way:

> That joke, that witty remark held on the tip of your tongue; the cheerful smile for those who annoy you; that silence when you're unjustly accused; your friendly conversation with people whom you find boring and tactless; the daily effort to overlook one irritating detail or another in the persons who live with you . . . this, with perseverance, is indeed solid interior mortification.*

Members of Opus Dei, like many other Christians and consistent with Church teachings, also practice a spirit of penance more akin to fasting and sometimes referred to as

---

*St. Josemaría Escrivá, *The Way* (New York: Scepter Publishers, 1985), no. 173.

corporal mortification. This practice involves offering up to God some of the discomforts that come with everyday life, for example, climbing stairs instead of taking an elevator, waiting a few minutes to drink water when they are thirsty, eating less of a food that they enjoy. This practice reminds them in a small way of the cross Jesus carried and died on to save us. Living this discipline also strengthens one's character and prepares one to face well the difficulties we all encounter in life. Indeed, it helps one to persevere in times of trial.

For the most part, each person decides what is most appropriate given his or her circumstances. The celibate members of Opus Dei, that is, the numeraries, numerary assistants, and associates, ordinarily use the cilice a couple of hours a day and the discipline once a week for the length of a prayer. These customs of penance were practiced by many of the saints throughout the Church's history, including St. Paul, St. Thomas More, as well as Mother Teresa and Padre Pio in our own times.

> And all who believed were together and had all things in common; and they sold their possessions and goods and distributed them to all, as any had need. And day by day, attending the temple together and breaking bread in their homes, they partook of food with glad and generous hearts, praising God and having favor with all people. (Acts 2:44–47)

As mentioned earlier, St. Josemaría likened Opus Dei's spirit and approach to the lifestyle of the early Christians, who were ordinary people in their social milieu and their work life. What differentiated them was their belief in Jesus

Christ, their charity with each other as well as with non-believers, and their commitment to living a virtuous life patterned on the life of Jesus Christ.

In their quest for holiness, members of Opus Dei strive to live all the Christian virtues and realize that this is a life-long task and work of grace that God must bring about in their souls. But their cooperation with that grace is required. Moreover, they are encouraged to approach their daily struggles with a sporting spirit, aware that they will need to begin again and again in their quest — like little children learning to walk, who tumble over so easily, and then bounce right back up.

> Earthly goods are not bad, but they are debased when man sets them up as idols, when he adores them. They are ennobled when they are converted into instruments for good, for just and charitable Christian undertakings. We cannot seek after material goods as if they were a treasure. . . . Our treasure is Christ and all our love and desire must be centered on him, "for where our treasure is, there will our hearts be also.*

All the members of Opus Dei strive to live the spirit of poverty and detachment, each one according to his or her personal circumstances. All members of Opus Dei are expected to work and support themselves from their earnings.

---

*St. Josemaría Escrivá, *Christ Is Passing By* (New York: Scepter Publishers, 1974), no. 35.

TWENTY

What Happened?

From Atheistic Radical Feminist
to Stay-at-Home Catholic Mom

I (Cindy Simmons) have been a member of Opus Dei for almost seventeen years. It enriches all aspects of my life by helping me understand everything with a supernatural outlook. In joining Opus Dei I did not change what I believed. Rather, being a member helps me to live my faith every day, and even every minute of every day. I consider everything in light of my faith. Everything I do, I do for the greater glory of God. I can't be lazy in my work or less than a sincere and loyal friend (no gossip!). If I have a hard day, I view it as an opportunity to give more glory to God by living it well, even when I feel awful. If I get bad news, I know that the news itself is not as important as how I react and handle it.

I love Mother Teresa's teaching that it is not what we do that is important to God but how we try. This is a far cry from how I was raised, where intelligence and success (mostly material) were of primary importance and happiness totally dependent on them.

I grew up in the 1960s and 1970s, graduating high school in 1975 and college in 1979. My family was well educated and well informed. I remember my mom and aunts talking about "women's lib" when I was about eight years old.

By the time I was in high school the women's liberation movement was well established and accepted by my affluent culturally Jewish community. I naturally had an independent spirit and embraced the feminism of the sixties that said I should rely entirely on myself. Men were superfluous and religion unnecessary. I saw religion as a crutch and antithetical to my independent spirit. Certainly a religion like Catholicism, "run by men," did not fit into my feminist ideals.

Part of my mind-set was formed by my parents' divorce in 1972 at the height of "No Fault" divorce. My mother, left by her husband of twenty-five years to fend for herself after devoting her life to her family, stressed to my sister and me the importance of self-reliance. Women cannot depend on husbands anymore. I entered adulthood with the vision that I would support myself through a meaningful career. Marriage was not a goal. I never wanted or needed a boyfriend to feel important. I sought out female friends who were also "strong women" and shared my viewpoint. It wasn't that we didn't like guys; we did. But we certainly didn't look to them for our salvation or support. If we did have boyfriends or husbands they were to be totally equal partners. My fulfillment was to be had through my career. Even if I did fall in love, marriage and children were not to be the defining features of my life. I would never be "just" a housewife.

In addition to self-reliance my other theme was truth. As it was for Mohandas Gandhi, "The passion for truth was innate in me." But I thought, "How can anyone know the truth?" I saw many different religions, all claiming the truth, and I saw many sinners in all of these religions. I had only weak religious training and I became an atheist at a young age. I had to find something other than religion on which to base the truth. In high school I developed a passion for science. It provided answers. I foolishly thought that complete understanding of the physical world could answer all questions, including moral questions. This fallacy was enforced when I started reading Ayn Rand. Her philosophy of Objectivism was in total conformity with my views. Like Hank Reardon in *Atlas Shrugged* I subscribed to the foolish notion that physical laws are a moral absolute.

I remember in college one of my science profs asked my microbiology class (about four hundred students) if we thought that everything could be explained by the material world. Most of us raised our hands. Of course, the logical conclusion of this is that man has no free will. If we are just chemicals whose reactions are solely governed by the laws of nature, how can there be any true decision making or moral choices? If I had been thinking more clearly at the time, I would have seen the absurdity of my position, that is, that man is free but Nature rules! My belief in truth and my belief that man has reason and free will to pursue it ultimately led me to my belief in God and in the Catholic Church.

I graduated with an M.S. in biochemistry from the University of Minnesota in 1983 and moved to the Bay Area. My sister lived there and the area was booming in my field of genetic engineering/molecular biology. I met my husband my first day in California. We spent a lot of our time together discussing deep issues we were both interested in, although we had (seemingly) wildly different viewpoints. He was a Christian and considering becoming Catholic. I remember thinking and even telling him, *"No! Don't do that, anything but Catholic!"* Christianity was bad enough without being Catholic. At twenty-five I was still in my atheist, feminist mind-set, and I just did not see how Catholicism could possibly fit in with my feminist ideals.

Fortunately, Lance was patient with my misconceptions about Catholicism, religion, and God. He first had to break down my resistance to God. This wasn't hard since I already believed in truth, and he was studying philosophy. It is a quick and compelling argument from truth to God. We married the summer after Lance entered the Catholic Church, one year after we met. Lance married me even though I barely believed in God and certainly was not a Catholic, and not planning on becoming one. My prejudice against the Church was still too strong.

From God to Jesus, and from Jesus to the Catholic Church was grace. We had many discussions about philosophy, religion, God, atheism. It was a difficult journey for me to overcome my bias against the Church. But I was eventually convinced of the truth of the Church. At the time I would have told you it was reason alone. My husband is a brilliant philosopher, and his arguments were compelling. Now I realize that many prayers (offered by my husband and friends) and grace were what led my hardened heart to open up to the Catholic Church.

One of the obstacles I faced in accepting the Church was its stance on abortion. How dare a bunch of celibate men tell women what to do with their bodies? It took me some time to overcome my initial repugnance and see that the Church's position was actually quite feminist and pro-woman. One of the feminist mandates is that women, while possibly physically weaker, are equal and should be treated equally. Weakness alone shouldn't condemn a person to an inferior position in society. I failed to extend this argument to the unborn child. The "fetus" was an obstacle to my freedom. Abortion was touted by the radical feminists as a tool that would help women be liberated. But what I saw was exactly the opposite. Rather than liberating women, abortion was a tool for their exploitation.

The sexual revolution did not liberate women but rather helped enslave them. Contraception encourages the idea in men that women should always be available. Contraception paved the way for the reality of sexual relationships without any requirement of responsibility or commitment.

Every friend I knew who had an abortion was coerced into it by her boyfriend. All these women were undergoing abortions, not through their own choice primarily but the choice of their men. And these were my "strong women" friends — women you would expect to be more thoughtful, strong, and immune to coercion. But I saw their decision was strongly influenced by what their partners wanted, contrary to their own more maternal inclinations.

I entered the Catholic Church at Easter Vigil in 1986. I can't say exactly at what point I went beyond believing what the Church teaches to loving my faith. The richness, the beauty, the truth, and above all, the grace help me every day to rejoice in my faith and strive to live it better. My life is completely different from what it would have been had I not converted. I am married with seven children and am very happy to see marriage as my vocation, my path to God. While this path is not always easy, I can't imagine being happier in any other life.

During the early years after my conversion I was like many new converts, quite enthusiastic and happy in my newfound faith. I wanted to be a good Catholic. I had good friends who steered me in the right direction. But because we are human, it is inevitable that the passion a new convert feels diminishes after a time. My enthusiasm was at times quite high, but then I would sink into a period of lukewarmness. I did not know how to channel my love for God into a concrete plan of life that would help me to persevere in cultivating my interior life,* regardless of my enthusiasm or dryness. Opus Dei helped me with that.

My husband and I moved to Notre Dame (South Bend, Indiana) in August 1986 so he could pursue a Ph.D. in philosophy. One of his fellow graduate students invited him to an activity sponsored by Opus Dei. He told me about the women's activities, and I started attending the evenings of recollection. I didn't always feel like going, but once I was there I was always very grateful to hear the meditations and talks on spirituality. They helped me tremendously to understand my faith and to incorporate it into my life. The solid doctrine and encouragement to foster your interior life were just what I needed. Here was a plan of life that would help me do exactly what I knew I should be doing. Sure, as a Catholic I knew I should pray. But when? How?

Opus Dei helped me to forge a concrete plan that I could follow. For example, I started to read the New Testament for five minutes every day. I would start with St. Matthew and about six months later I would be finished with Revelation and start over again. It was amazing how this helped me. I started to know Our Lord and love him. From such a simple easy thing that only took five minutes.

One of the main attractions I felt for Opus Dei was its emphasis on apostolate, that is, bringing the message of Jesus

---

*Interior Life: The personal life of prayer, the inner intimacy that an individual enjoys with God.

Christ to the world. As a convert myself I understood that all people, no matter how far from God they may appear, are never a lost cause. I certainly would never have predicted that I would be a believer, let alone a devout Catholic. And while Opus Dei does emphasize apostolate, St. Josemaría also insisted that we respect individuals. People have a right to believe what they will, and we cannot force anyone to our viewpoint. My apostolate was to be an apostolate of friendship. I prayed for my friends and family, but I rarely brought up my beliefs because I knew that would not be appreciated. I was always happy when they asked me questions, but because my Jewish family was quite resistant to Christianity, I had to respect that they did not agree with me and had the right not to talk about it.

It seems so simple from the outside: doctrine, prayer. But to really live a contemplative life in the midst of the world is difficult. Our human frailties make it quite easy to offer excuses for not going to Mass or saying our prayers. We are very busy and cannot always get to our prayers. Opus Dei helps us overcome the everyday obstacles that would keep us from God. Without the help of Opus Dei, I could not do it. Opus Dei helps me to live my goal of loving God every minute of the day. Whether I am actively praying or involved in the daily routines of my life, I can always lift any activity to God. I am very grateful that God saw fit to give St. Josemaría the vision, mission, and grace to found Opus Dei. My vocation to Opus Dei gives me the grace and helps me to persevere in my path to sanctity.

TWENTY-ONE

Apostolic Celibacy

The main difference between the supernumerary members of Opus Dei and the numerary, numerary assistant, and associate members of Opus Dei is that the latter group have received a call to "apostolic celibacy." They dedicate their whole lives to God in order to put themselves at the service of the apostolates of Opus Dei (that is, evangelical efforts and organized programs). This calling represents a special, personal invitation from God to choose him alone to serve and love. A married person seeks holiness and union with God through loving and giving oneself to one's spouse. Women and men who receive a celibate vocation to Opus Dei are more available to receive their formation more intensively and are able to staff Opus Dei activities more easily.

The tradition of celibacy within the Catholic Church was lived by Jesus himself, St. John the Baptist, St. John the apostle, and St. Paul. From the earliest times of the Catholic Church, there has been a tradition of men and women receiving and living out vocations to celibacy.

Celibate persons in Opus Dei give their hearts completely to Jesus Christ, specifically by serving souls in and through their work and through the formational activities and programs of Opus Dei. Numeraries, numerary assistants, and associates in Opus Dei freely commit themselves to this calling after they have prayed much about it and sought spiritual direction on the matter. They each must choose to renew their dedication once a year for the first five years after they have agreed to live this dedication. After that, if they wish, they make a lifetime commitment. Members of Opus Dei, whether celibate or not, are not "consecrated" as religious are, but remain ordinary lay people.

They are persons who are called to serve other souls in a particular way and firmly believe that their gift of self to others enables them to engender the spirit of Christ in the souls they serve and all the souls in their life.

TWENTY-TWO

Finding a Vocation

Interview with a Hospitality Professional

Q: Can you share a bit about yourself? Where you're from, what you do?

Pat Duryea: I'm from Chicago. I was born on the North Side. I'm fifty-five years old. I've been in Opus Dei for thirty-seven years. I'm a numerary assistant. This means two things: it means I'm totally dedicated to God, and I have chosen as my profession the care of my family of Opus Dei.

Q: Can you explain a little more about the concept of vocation?

Pat: Sometimes people think that their professional vocation is something they just chose. They were in high school and they loved biology, and maybe they loved people, so they thought about being a doctor. And they think it's all up to them, but really it's like God leading them on the path professionally as well. He has some role he wants you to play.

Q: Is this for people in Opus Dei or people in general?

Pat: People in general. I think God's leading everybody along a path. And maybe they don't realize it, or maybe they say no, so they've deviated from the very beginning of what God had in mind. So he creates everyone for a purpose. I never thought about this until lately, when I started to reflect as I went through middle age.

Q: What did you think you would do in the beginning?

Pat: My first professional choice was history, American history. I really was convinced that what I wanted to do was to study American history and teach American history. I think because of two teachers I had in high school and then a professor in my first year of college, I was just enamored with it. And then I realized that it wasn't all it was built up to be. I was disillusioned.

Q: Why? How did you discover that?

Pat: The people I thought were patriots were human; they weren't superheroes. I think I was an absolute patriot, and then I came to realize that America had a lot of defects. And I also discovered what I like to do is to work with people, and that if I wanted to study history, it was going to be maybe six years or so, very serious studying by myself. And I really wanted to deal more with people.

Then a lot happened in my life that changed my path. When I was a freshman in college, my father died suddenly of heart disease. I had to take over the role in my family of helping my mother. My other two sisters were married. I had one younger brother, and I was the most responsible person around. So I gave my mother a hand. I decided to drop out of school, and I got a job in a brokerage house in the accounting department. I discovered I loved business. I started to have a life, a salary, and I just loved that. I loved working downtown. I loved my friends. I loved everything, and I wasn't giving much consideration to going back to school. I was just having a great time.

But then God intervened in my life again. I had found out about Opus Dei. With the death of my father, I went through a hard time, and so did my mother. My mother basically lost her faith for a while. It was hard for her to accept the loss of my father. One of the priests of Opus Dei really helped me see that God's not a hunter, that God takes people when they're ready. He really helped me go through that struggle I had in my life, and his intervention brought me close to God, close to my faith, and very close to Opus Dei. The people I met at the center were also a big help. The center was only twenty minutes' walk from my house. For years I didn't know it was there.

Q: Did you go to the center a lot? What's a center of Opus Dei like? Could you describe it? Are they all the same?

Pat: Oh no, they're all very different. This was an old house, a very big old family house on the North Side, close to Lake Michigan, about a block away from the beach. It was a five- or six-bedroom house, big living room, formal dining room. It was a very nice house. And a lot of very interesting people lived there. There were foreigners who lived there, and I didn't know any foreigners, so it was fun. There were, I know, a couple of Spaniards, and I just loved all those people who lived there. They were so nice to me. It was such a family there.

Early on I brought one of my sisters to some activity there, and she told me, "Either these people are faking it, or they are totally happy." And it was true they were totally happy; nobody was faking it. She could see that.

Q: When did you find out about Opus Dei?

In 1967 I was a senior in high school, and a friend of mine invited me to go on a retreat to Shellbourne, a conference center of Opus Dei in Indiana. In our senior year, we all had to go on a retreat. It was a requirement of the school before you graduated. She had asked every single person in our clique, which was a lot of people. We were about ten girls. And everyone had said no, and I knew that, so when she asked me I hemmed and hawed and finally I said yes. And that changed my whole life.

I went on that retreat and the priest — his name was Father Sal — was really interested in me when I went to talk to him. On the day I went on the retreat I had just gotten my first rejection letter from college. I hadn't told anyone. He asked me if I was happy, and I started to cry. I wasn't happy at all, and he was so concerned for me and so fatherly to me, I could feel it.

I kept going to Father Sal to talk to him. He was giving me a lot of help, and I attended other classes of Christian formation as well.

I had set a date for myself, that by Christmas I would decide if I was going to be in Opus Dei or not. And they said, "Well, what did you decide?" And I said, "Yes, I want to be in Opus Dei." So right then I joined Opus Dei. I became a supernumerary.

So my life had changed. My father had died. I had to quit school. Now I was a supernumerary member of Opus Dei.

I was so grateful. I was getting a tremendous amount of support.

At that center of Opus Dei they were organizing a trip to Rome to see the Pope, to live Holy Week in Rome, and to see the founder of Opus Dei. It didn't cost a lot of money. I had enough money in the bank, so I told my mom, "What do you think?" And she said, "Go for it."

So I went and I had that opportunity to see Pope Paul VI. I mean, my gosh, I was impressed. It was the first time in my life I had ever gone to all the Easter services — Holy Thursday, Good Friday, Holy Saturday. And there I was with the Pope doing those things.

Q: Did you meet St. Josemaría?

Pat: I did. I didn't get to greet him personally. I was in a gathering of young people from the United States, Ireland, and Kenya, three English-speaking countries, a very diverse group of people. I could see that he was a saint from the moment he walked in the room.

I realized that if God gave me this great big gift, of meeting the Pope, of meeting St. Josemaría, that gift demanded a response. God wanted something else from my life.

That afternoon, after I had seen the founder, a person from Chicago who was living in Rome met up with me. We went for a long walk in Villa Borghese (a beautiful park in Rome) and talked and talked. "What would God want — what else could I do for God?" Maybe God wanted my whole life. I was at that point very much convinced of it. But what do I do with my mother? I had the big responsibility of taking care of her and the family situation.

I came back to the States and went to talk to the director of the center. She told me what it meant to be an associate member of Opus Dei, and it seemed to fit all my circumstances. Within a short period of time I asked to become an associate. And I remained an associate for almost seven years, going through a lot of career changes. I never could find professionally what I really wanted to do. And at one point I contracted hepatitis. I had to have surgery. I was very sick for almost a whole year.

Gabriela Duclaud was the director of Opus Dei for women in the Chicago area. She was a woman with an incredible heart, an incredible generosity. She came to visit me in the hospital. Right when I was going to get out of the hospital, they told me to go home and rest for a couple of months and then they would see how I was doing. Gabriela knew what a burden it would be for my mother if I went home and rested at home. My mother was working full-time. How would she take care of me? So Gabriela told me, "Why don't you go to Shellbourne and live in the administration?"

Q: What is an administration?

Pat: It's the part of the conference center where the live-in staff live and work.

Q: There's a live-in staff for the conference centers?

Pat: Yes, for this one. There were only three people who were the live-in staff at the time, and then a tremendous number of day employees who really run the place.

She said, "Why don't you go there and rest? They don't have any activities there. They'll take care of you, and don't worry about it."

So I went home from the hospital and went to Shell-bourne. They picked me up and took me out there. It was like going to a resort. I think I was in bed almost the entire time I was there.

They brought me a tray three times a day, with a little flower and a candle at night for the dinner. I was so impressed with it. And they were running around like crazy. There were only three of them. And here they were, taking care of me. And then I realized what it meant to live a life dedicated to serving people. I really was enamored with that, the generosity of those people who took care of me. They took care of me as if they were my mother, besides everything else they had to do. When I returned home from my time there, within a few weeks I was back in the hospital, I had to have my gallbladder removed, and I had pneumonia. I was really sick.

Somehow amid my sickness and the exquisite care I received, I realized that what I really wanted to do was to go work in the administrations of the centers of Opus Dei.

And when I went to the director of the center, she said, "No, wait. You don't have any background. You have to support your family. You have to finish school, et cetera." And I said, "What if I get a job in the industry and see if it's really for me? And then I'll see if I can find a culinary school I can attend here in Chicago part-time because I need to work full-time." So I really had no idea, but I knew that the best place to learn would be in a hotel kitchen.

So I went to all the big hotels in Chicago, and I tried to get a job in the kitchens, but they wouldn't hire me because it was around 1973, and none of those big kitchens had women, none of them. It's all unionized, and the work is heavy. That's one excuse they gave me for why there were no women there. The other excuse was that the atmosphere is not very agreeable for a woman. But they offered me a job on the front desk. It was at the Palmer House, which is a Hilton hotel in Chicago.

I started to work there, and as soon as I got the job I started to look for culinary schools, but there weren't any in Chicago. The best culinary school I could go to would have been the Culinary Institute of America in Hyde Park, New York. Although I needed to live at home, that was my dream. That was where I wanted to go to school. But I couldn't do it. Nothing was going to work for me. So I just continued working. I worked for a couple of years, and I went back to college, figuring I could get my degree at the same time, so I took courses here and there. I liked the front desk. I got promoted to front desk supervisor for one of the shifts. It was a big hotel, very busy. I had a nice experience working there.

Then one of the centers of Opus Dei in Chicago needed workers. Someone had quit, and they needed somebody in a hurry. So they asked me, "Can you fill in over the weekend?" So I did that, and then I asked, "Don't you want me to work here full-time?" And they took me up on it.

They were very happy to have me. Some of the people who worked in that administration and in other administrations around there were people who had a lot of background and could teach me a lot of things. So I learned a lot as I worked. I was a studious person. I liked to read a lot. I read every issue of *Gourmet* magazine. *Gourmet* magazine started in 1955; I read every single one. So I was working there and having a great time. In the meantime, my mom was now more settled. She could handle her life on her own, and I made the big decision that I would move out of my family's home. I was already in my mid- to late twenties, and I got an apartment with some of my friends. There were four of us young women in that apartment. A couple of us were members of Opus Dei. We had a lot of friends come and go, move in, move out. It was great.

About that time Lexington College was founded. It was located very close to the campus of the University of Illinois on a little street called Lexington Avenue. Since I was studying accounting, they asked me if I would like to do the books for them. They were starting out and needed people who could do a little volunteer work. "Can you take care of this for us? Can you answer the phones?" Sure I could. I think I spent more time there than I did on my own campus! It was just the beginning, and I had a lot of fun.

At some point someone mentioned to me that maybe God was calling me to be a numerary assistant in Opus Dei.

I was already a celibate member of Opus Dei. It would mean moving to a center of Opus Dei, because I would become a numerary and not an associate, and the associate members of Opus Dei in general live in their family's homes or in their own apartments, not in the centers.

It's a matter of circumstances; it's not a matter of generosity. People live together in a center because you need to live as a family. You get support from living with other people who are trying to do what you're trying to do. Once you realize what the administration of Opus Dei centers is, then you realize why people would want to live there. I've been living in New York now for five years. I have a lot of single friends. When they realize the services we provide for the people who live in their center of the Opus Dei, they are like, "Wow."

Q: Do you think that the work you do is much like a stay-at-home mom's work?

Pat: On a professional level, yes, but I get paid a salary. The centers we take care of pay us a very good salary.

Q: And do you get benefits?

Pat: I get benefits. I have all my hospitalization paid for. I have four weeks off every year. I have a pretty good deal.

TWENTY-THREE

"Every Single Thing Matters to Him"

Interview with a Retired New York City Public School Teacher

Jeanne Murray has been an associate member of Opus Dei since 1975. Jeanne has been actively involved in the Rosedale Achievement Center, an inner-city supplemental education center for girls and women in the South Bronx, since 1978. An African American, retired New York City public school teacher, and former foster child, Jeanne brings passion and vision to Rosedale and her work with young girls from some of New York City's toughest neighborhoods.

Q: When did you meet Opus Dei?

Jeanne: I met Opus Dei when I was a student at Hunter College and Father Paul Donlan (a priest of Opus Dei) was the chaplain of the Newman Club.

Q: What year was that?

Jeanne: That was 1966; I was a sophomore.

Q: And you joined Opus Dei in 1975?

Jeanne: Well, it took me a while, yes.

Q: Is that normal? Is that how it works with most people in Opus Dei?

Jeanne: I don't think so. It took me a long while to believe that Opus Dei was as good as it was. I was a real skeptic.

Q: What made you skeptical?

Jeanne: I thought it was too good to be true. The prayer life. Going to Mass every day. Saying the rosary. Going to spiritual direction, to the meditations, retreats, and all of that. I thought, well, that's just ducky, but then there's a real world out there where people are yelling and screaming at each other and trying to get along with each other. It seemed like it was the ideal, but in the real world this was not what was happening. I tell you, one of the best moments was when I heard someone in an Opus Dei center yell at somebody else. These are real people, thank you very much!

Q: Did you ever get to meet St. Josemaría?

Jeanne: No. I went to Rome the spring after he died, in 1976.

Q: Were you a practicing Catholic when you met Opus Dei?

Jeanne: Yes, I have been a practicing Catholic my whole life.

Q: Tell me a little bit about your childhood? Some people might consider your childhood challenging.

Jeanne: Well, I'll tell you the truth, I lucked out. I had the best deal. Most foster kids go from family to family. I went to two families. When I was born my mother took me to the

New York Foundling Hospital. It used to be on Sixty-Eighth Street. Now it's downtown. So I was there for two years.

Q: At the hospital? Were you sick?

Jeanne: No. It's called a hospital, but it was really a home for kids. Cardinal Spellman started it. It was Catholic. So that was another great thing my mother did. She did not have an abortion. She was not married, and she was from out of the country, and in the neighborhood I grew up in it wasn't impossible to get an abortion — and that was sixty years ago. She took me there, and it was a Catholic institution. She wanted that. So when you're two years old they try to find you a foster home and then they ship you out.

Q: Did you know your mother at all?

Jeanne: Yes, I did. She used to come and visit, so from the time I was five or six I realized that the lady who came to visit from time to time was my mother.

Q: And what has happened to her?

Jeanne: She died in 1971. But I used to go visit her. When I was little she would come to our house, and then when I was in high school I used to go visit her. She worked at the U.N. and we'd meet after school.

Q: Did she ever marry and have a family?

Jeanne: No, she didn't.

Q: You were her only child?

Jeanne: Yes. She told me she never told her family about me. I felt sorry for her because it was something she carried with her through her life, for the most part by herself. She was from Haiti and had relatives in Washington, D.C. She was a journalist. Once I went to her house to visit her by surprise, but it wasn't totally a surprise because she had left her return address on a present she had sent me one year, and I saved it when I was a little kid.

Then when I got old enough I said, well, hmm, let me go investigate. She lived on Seventy-Second Street off Riverside Drive. I had asked her one time, "What if I come live with you?" I loved my foster parents; they were the best. But I tell you, if she had said, "Come home, my dear! Come home to live with me!" I would have. Because she was my mother.

She said, "Oh no, you could never live with me really." Because she had her job and her career, and she just couldn't take care of a kid. So I went to visit her one day and I rang the bell. You know how in the movies people say they see their life pass before them? Well, I was waiting at the bottom of the stairs, and it seemed like an eternity. She said, "Who is it?" I said who I was and she said, at the end of eternity, "Come up." Well, that was music to my ears. I went up. We had a really nice visit, and I said, "Well, you know I could come from time to time." And she said, "Oh no, you cannot come back."

She was glad I came. She said to me, "I knew some day you would come." That was good, but that was it, because she had other friends, and they didn't know about me. And she didn't want them to know about me. So we decided we would write to each other. I figured I could play tough too, so I said, "Don't write to me at home; write to me at school." And I gave her my school address. I was really mom and kid with my foster mother. I almost never said anything after I had met with my mother because my foster mother always seemed a little upset when I mentioned her.

Q: *She was jealous?*

Jeanne: Sort of, yes. She was my mother for all intents and purposes.

Q: *But she never adopted you.*

Jeanne: My biological mother wouldn't agree to it, amazingly enough.

Q: *How often did she come to visit you?*

Jeanne: I guess every couple of months, maybe once or twice a year. She would come when I was living with my foster family and later when I went to live with the Murrays. I changed my name when I was twenty-one. The Murrays really were my family, but I never said anything to my biological mother. It was not her concern; it was my choice. And it was the one thing I could do, to say to the Murrays, "Thank you. You guys took me as your kid."

Q: *Were they African American too?*

Jeanne: Yes.

Q: *Okay, tell me about the Murrays.*

Jeanne: My foster father was from St. Kitts [an island in the Caribbean]. He was raised Catholic. My foster mother converted. She had been a Presbyterian. She was from North Carolina. When my sister [foster sister, Vee] was born, they had been married about ten years and hadn't been able to have kids. And when she got pregnant with my sister, my foster father asked her if she would become a Catholic so they could raise Vee in the Catholic Church — one faith and one family. She agreed. The one thing she understood perfectly was Our Lady. She and the Blessed Mother were in cahoots. She understood clearly, and maybe that's where I learned to love Our Lady. My foster mother almost died; she was in the hospital for months after Vee was born because something went awry.

And then here I come on the scene. They had one happy little kid — Mom and Dad and a sweet little child. So why on earth? They said they wanted a playmate for Vee, because there wasn't going to be another child. I used to think, uh, a playmate. Well, I wish you'd just want me for me. However, that was the least of any foster kid's problems. They wanted me.

Q: Was your foster father the only father you've ever known?

Jeanne: Right.

Q: Tell me more about your foster mother.

Jeanne: Very loving. It took a while before she really, really wanted me. It was another kid. I think it's normal. I think it's wonderful that at some point she did say, "I love you as if you were my own," that she really did want me. But it was a challenge not to say anything to either one of them that could in any way be construed as my preferring one of my mothers over the other. In fact, one time my biological mother said something about not liking the way my hair was combed. I was a nice quiet little kid, but I almost lost it that time. Who on earth was she to complain about the way my hair is combed? Give me a break, lady. Anyway, I also remember trying to please my biological mother, trying to be very ladylike. And I took French in high school because she spoke French since she was from Haiti.

Q: What about your foster father?

Jeanne: He was a great guy. He taught me about God Our Father. I had done some cruddy things when I first came to live with them. My foster mother was really mad, but he just said to me, "Did you do that?" And I said, "Yes." He said, "Don't do that again." It was the end of it. He never ever said that again, and that was all he said. There was no yelling or screaming or whatever. That to me was what God is like; it was the best. He assumed the best about me and I was not a good kid. But he gave me the benefit of the doubt. I was in eighth grade when he died of a heart attack — two weeks before I turned thirteen.

Q: Are there many African Americans in Opus Dei in the United States?

Jeanne: Well, there are some. I wouldn't say a lot.

Q: There are a lot of black members in Africa, right?

Jeanne: That's right. Honestly, I wish there were more. I pray for that.

Q: Is that because there aren't many black Catholics in general?

Jeanne: That's the start of it, yes.

Q: Why are you in Opus Dei? What do you get out of it?

Jeanne: I'm glad you ask that question because there's no end to what I get. It's the same reason I have for being a Catholic. Somebody used to say, You don't go to Mass to get something; you go to give something. And I think all of that goes together. I go to Mass to adore God, to thank him, to ask him for things. To make up for things, make reparation. And he gives me all the things I need to live this life he has given me. I remember when I was in college and I first started hanging out with Opus Dei. Part of it was that I needed to learn how to live without being angry so much of the time. Even when I started teaching, I remember thinking, I'm going to either be in jail or dead because I couldn't believe how angry I could get.

And that was what impressed me about Father Paul Donlan, the priest of Opus Dei, one of the chaplains for the Newman Club at Hunter College. He never argued over anything. He would say whatever he had to say, calmly, politely, rationally, and that was it. If you had a question, or comment, that was wonderful.

When I got to Hunter, I went to the Newman Club because I missed the Catholic life. When I was in kindergarten and first grade in Brooklyn, I went to public school, but other than that I went to a Catholic elementary school and high school.

In April of 1968 Dr. Martin Luther King Jr. was assassinated; then Robert F. Kennedy (RFK) was assassinated in June of '68, and that's when I was ready to chuck it all. I went to a dinner at the Newman Club around then; every year the juniors in the Newman Club would have a special dinner to say good-bye to the seniors. It was the beginning of June, and it was after RFK was assassinated. Someone said, "What a lovely evening," and I started to cry. I was so mortified. In the Newman Club, I was the tough New Yorker. I couldn't believe I would actually cry in front of all these people!

The façade fell. I asked one of the parish priests, nuns, different people: What is all of this about? What is life all about? This is crazy. These people are dead; they stood for something good, in my opinion, and they're dead. And people are shopping, they're going in and out of Lord & Taylor's and Saks Fifth Avenue — just like nothing ever happened. What is this? And Father Paul was the only one who answered my question. I don't remember his exact words, but he said, "Here, take this piece of paper. This is the name of the person who is the director of the Opus Dei center on Seventieth Street. Joanne Angelo. Go and talk to her, and she'll give you some ideas of what you can do." That was the start of the whole thing with Opus Dei.

I went there. The meditation and spiritual direction were wonderful. They made a difference. And when you ask what has Opus Dei done for me, it is the avenue; it is my whole life. It takes all that God has given me — I don't drive very well, I don't cook very well, I don't do anything very well. I can teach, that's the thing I do best, and I'm not the star teacher either. All that God has given me, Opus Dei is an avenue, a channel, to give it back. That's it. That's the bottom line.

Q: You're an associate member of Opus Dei. What does that mean? What makes an associate different from a numerary or a supernumerary member of Opus Dei? And how did you know that was the right one for you?

Jeanne: Numeraries usually live in the center, and the associates don't. Supernumeraries live at home; associates do too. Supernumeraries may be married or get married and associates don't have that plan because that's not God's plan for us. That came again from asking God, "All right. What do you want?"

At that point I was living with my foster mother, who had never lived alone. Even when she came to New York from the South, she lived with roommates and then she got married. For her to live alone — she was in her seventies then — would have been a real hardship. I thought that's what God wanted, that I look out for her.

A few weeks before my father died, we went on our first, last, and only family vacation to Saratoga. He was sick. My sister and I thought he had ulcers, because that's what they told us. Actually he had a heart problem. It was late at night. We were on the train, and my sister and I were sitting in front of them. Probably they thought we were asleep. I was not asleep. I heard my mother say to him, "What am I going to do without you?" He said to her, "Don't worry, they're girls, they'll stay with you. They won't leave you." I could have been asleep and not heard that. The fact that I did hear it meant, to me, that that was what God wanted. That was it.

Q: What does an associate do? What's your life like? What does it mean to be an associate?

Jeanne: Associates can give more time to the activities and the needs of Opus Dei than supernumeraries can, for the most part, because we don't have a family at home per se. Some associates do live with their parents or other members

of their family. We have more time than most supernumeraries, but often not as much as the numeraries, who are
responsible for all the activities in the center. I worked full
time until I retired, but on the weekends for twenty years,
I worked with the Rosedale girls club in the Bronx. I had
time to do that because I wasn't taking care of a husband
or kids of my own. It's funny because every now and then I
have a conversation either with the kids themselves or their
parents, and they will ask me, "So why aren't you married?"
And I say, "Because not being married makes it possible for
me to be here on Saturdays to help take care of the kids in
the program when many moms can't be doing that." There
are some people God asks to do that.

**Q: Mass every day, rosary every day, you take courses
every year during your vacation time to study theology
pretty rigorously. Some people think that's demanding.
Was that hard to adapt to?**

Jeanne: For me it was harder to adapt to growing in virtue.
The other stuff is the fuel for the fire. I would want Mass
every day.

**Q: How do you think your vocation to Opus Dei influenced
you as a teacher?**

Jeanne: I think, professionally, trying to do this job the
best I could, taking classes and courses, learning from other
people, asking advice. Knowing there's a better way to do
this and making the effort to find the better way.

Q: Did you also pray for your kids?

Jeanne: Absolutely, absolutely. It's very bad if a kid knows that a teacher's afraid of him or her. And I remember being afraid of one kid and thinking, I don't have the courage to deal with this and I need it — for that kid's sake and for everybody else's sake, because otherwise the kid was going to run the show. There is no way I could not have prayed for those kids, no way I could not have gone to Mass every day. That's what gave me the fuel to deal with the situation.

Q: You're a retired New York City public school teacher. What do you do with your time now?

Jeanne: I help Rosedale with the girls' program. I also help train other young people, some of whom are teachers or are thinking about teaching or working with the summer program. A lot of time also goes into helping the parents see how to teach their kids, how to deal with them. There is so much in life that is a hassle, just living life. It's not enough for me to teach the kids. It's also important to teach the parents, so that the parents can teach their kids. Sometimes the kids lose respect for their parents because they think the parents don't know.

The parents sometimes are so burdened by other things that they are tempted to take the easy way out — let the school teach them. There's so much of this job that is the parent's. After I retired I started a preschool program, through Rosedale, and a parent or grandparent had to come. We met twice a week for two hours. It was called Reading Readiness. Now we're out of space and out of people, so I work with the older kids.

The core of that program was to help the parents see what they ordinarily do in life that can be used as educational opportunities for their kids — like walking down the street and talking to the kids, having a conversation. "Sit down," "Stop it," "I told you not to touch that" — these are not conversations! The kids should go to school knowing their whole name, their address, how old they are, the numbers, the letters, the colors. That's from home. When kids don't learn these things until they're five or six years old, in school, then we have that well-known achievement gap. They are left behind. The program was intended to help the parents teach their kids, and it's a joy. The first time one kid's parent read a story to the class, the kid was mesmerized, just staring at his mom reading a book to him.

Q: How do you think Opus Dei as an organization has changed since you joined?

Jeanne: There are many more people in Opus Dei, and I honestly think that it's more appreciated. More people know about the Work and appreciate the idea of sanctifying your life, of giving your life to God, of helping other people.

Q: If you knew someone was thinking about joining Opus Dei, what would you tell that person?

Jeanne: Pray, pray a lot. Talk to somebody, talk to a priest, talk to a member of Opus Dei, and get involved. Go to meditations.

Q: Looking back on your life, how do you think your life has benefited from being in Opus Dei?

Jeanne: I believe that God is the center of my life, and I don't think that would be the case otherwise. I appreciate what life is and understand that God has a plan for us, that God is our Father. He is part of every single thing, not just Sunday morning from 9:00 to 10:00 a.m. That it's all day every day. Every single thing matters to him, and he loves us.

TWENTY-FOUR

Conclusion

This book has attempted to provide readers with testi-monies of a cross-section of women in Opus Dei. They are as varied in their religious upbringing as they are in their ethnic backgrounds. Some of the women are "cradle Catholics," while others converted to Catholicism and then discovered their calling to Opus Dei. One of the women was previously an atheist. Several of the women are Hispanic, several African American, several Asian. Professionally, sev-eral of the women are at the top of their fields: one a renowned scientist and another a chief marketing officer for a multinational corporation. Five of the women have the maintaining of their homes and families as their pro-fessional work. One of the women runs a family childcare business from her home.

While most of the women in the book are married and with children, six of those featured are celibate. Each woman has her own unique story, and yet they share some things in common. Most of the women discovered their call-ing to Opus Dei after having attended Opus Dei programs for some years. They usually found out about Opus Dei either through a relative, a spouse, or a friend. They all are in love with their Catholic faith and see Opus Dei as a way to live that faith better, thereby loving God and other souls more earnestly. They all agree that their vocation to Opus

Dei somehow gives them more sense of purpose and satis-faction in their work and social relations. They all seem to enjoy a sense of certainty that God loves them deeply, and they therefore appear to have in common a sense of peace about what their life means.

What readers do not find among the women in the book are shared political views. They all have their personal opinions about politics, economic theories, and educational philosophy; they have their own preferences, with respect to fashion, art, literature, music, and film. They enjoy a broad diversity and pluralism. Really, what unites all these women is their love for God and their desire to live that love and life of faith in a consistent, secular, and Catholic way as they go about the ordinary events of their everyday life.

If readers would like to find out more about Opus Dei we suggest they visit Opus Dei's website: *www.opusdei.org.* Readers who want to read more profiles and articles specif-ically about women in Opus Dei and related topics, please visit *www.womanandwork.org,* published by Bayridge Res-idence, a student residence in Boston. We also suggest that readers look into books by St. Josemaría Escrivá. Please visit *www.escrivaworks.org* for a complete list of St. Josemaría's works as well as the possibility for viewing on-line ex-cerpts from each book. Scott Hahn's book, *Ordinary Work, Extraordinary Grace: My Spiritual Journey in Opus Dei* (Doubleday Religion, 2006), might prove an interesting read for those interested in learning more from a member's point of view.

We end with this quotation from St. Josemaría, which we believe summarizes one of the most powerful attractions of Opus Dei:

God is calling you to serve Him in and from the ordinary, material and secular activities of human life. He waits for us every day, in the laboratory, in the operating theatre, in the army barracks, in the university chair, in the factory, in the workshop, in the fields, in the home and in all the immense panorama of work. Understand this well: there is something holy, something divine, hidden in the most ordinary situations, and it is up to each one of you to discover it. (St. Josemaría Escrivá, from his homily entitled "Passionately Loving the World," which can be found in the book *Conversations*)

George Weigel
AGAINST THE GRAIN
Christianity and Democracy, War and Peace

Cutting against the grain of conventional wisdom, *New York Times* bestseller George Weigel offers a compelling look at the ways in which Catholic social teaching sheds light on the challenges of peace, the problem of pluralism, the quest for human rights, and the defense of liberty. Weigel offers a meticulous analysis of the foundations of the free society as he makes a powerful case for the role of moral reasoning in meeting the threats to human dignity posed by debonair nihilism, jihadist violence, and the brave new world of manufactured men and women.

"*Against the Grain* will be invaluable to all who ponder how to bring Christian social teachings to bear on the most urgent political, economic, and cultural issues in contemporary life. In these marvelously readable essays, Weigel challenges reigning opinion on a wide range of issues, offers fresh insights drawn from the Catholic intellectual heritage, and opens a conversation 'with all partisans of the free and virtuous society, of whatever creed or no creed.' "

— MARY ANN GLENDON, Professor of Law,
Harvard University

978-0-8245-2448-7, hardcover

crossroad

George William Rutler
COINCIDENTALLY

From the Da Vinci Code and Roswell to E Pluribus Unum and the pyramid on the back of every dollar bill, we all are fascinated by secrets, codes, and coincidences. George Rutler — EWTN speaker, *Crisis* magazine columnist, and reigning Catholic wit — offers his reflections on the coincidental links that connect the most far-flung parts of our worlds. Topics cover the gamut of human life, from Louis Farrakhan and Edgar Allan Poe to Benjamin Franklin and the propensity of Scottish physicians to dominate the Nobel Prizes for Medicine.

Fr. George Rutler is best known as the host of a weekly program on EWTN and the pastor of Our Saviour in midtown New York City, where he lives.

0-8245-2440-3, hardcover

Check your local bookstore for availability.
To order directly from the publisher,
please call 1-800-707-0670 for Customer Service
or visit our website at *www.cpcbooks.com.*

crossroad